# THE
# WASHINGTON
# ARSENAL
# EXPLOSION

## Civil War Disaster in the Capital

## BRIAN BERGIN

### EDITED BY ERIN BERGIN VOORHEIS
### FOREWORD BY STEVE HAMMOND

Charleston   London

THE
History
PRESS

Published by The History Press
Charleston, SC 29403
www.historypress.net

*Front cover*: Ruins of the Washington Arsenal Laboratory after the June 17, 1864 explosion.
*Courtesy of National Defense University, Library Directorate, Fort McNair, Washington, D.C.*
*Back cover, top*: The monument to the women killed in the Washington Arsenal explosion.
*Congressional Cemetery, Washington, D.C. Photo by Brian Bergin.*
*Back cover, bottom*: Arsenal workers on the porch of the Washington Arsenal laboratory. *The
Washington Arsenal Manufactory Women Killed in the Explosion, 1864 (circa): National Archives and
Records Administration, College Park, MD, Still Photo Division.*

First published 2012

Manufactured in the United States

ISBN 978.1.60949.793.4

Library of Congress CIP data applied for.

# CONTENTS

# FOREWORD

When I began leading tours at Congressional Cemetery in 2006, I quickly realized that even though the military aspects of the Civil War are well documented, less is understood about civilian lives in wartime Washington and especially how women were affected by the war.

One of the cemetery's focal points is the monument to the victims of the 1864 Arsenal explosion, a catastrophe that in its day had an impact felt across the country.

Although a marker at Fort McNair was placed in 1998 to note the event, the Arsenal explosion has been barely a footnote in the broader narrative of the Civil War. The nation has largely forgotten those twenty-one young women, some of whom were just teenagers, who died working to protect the Union at a time when few women worked outside their homes or sought jobs beyond domestic service. I found I had to know more about the event and, more importantly, about the young women whose sacrifice and suffering equaled that of many battlefield soldiers. How could this city and nation forget those twenty-one women?

Then Brian Bergin contacted the cemetery office indicating that he was working on a book about the explosion. Over the next several months, I was in regular contact with Brian as I pulled and copied files from the cemetery's archives for him. As we talked and e-mailed, I realized that Brian's work would be an important contribution to the body of knowledge about Washington in the Civil War.

In the fall of 2008, Brian came to do research and visit the monuments in the cemetery. I had the pleasure of showing him around the grounds. We had lunch together, and I drove him to nearby Mount Olivet Cemetery, where four of the Arsenal victims lie together in an unmarked grave and the sculptor Lot Flannery, who created the monument at Congressional Cemetery, also takes his final rest. It was the only time we ever met in person, and I'm grateful for the few short hours we spent together that day.

In July 2009, as Brian was looking for a publisher for this book and preparing to give a face to this tragedy, a heart problem claimed him. Since that time, his daughter, Erin Bergin Voorheis, has worked to get the book published. She felt, as I do, that this is a story that the nation should know. Brian relates how these young women, all from the working class of Washington, overcame various adversities to get by in a city torn by partisan sentiment. He helps us understand what life was like for them and the sacrifices they made to help their families and serve their country.

I wish I had had an opportunity to get to know Brian better, but it has been an honor to play a role in developing this book and to work with Erin to see it come to print. With its meticulous research and articulate narrative, it is a fitting legacy for Brian. It adds immeasurably to the body of knowledge about the Civil War and shows that even a century and a half later there is still much to be learned about the events of the conflict that played such a crucial role in shaping our nation.

Well done, Brian. Well done.

Steve Hammond
Washington, D.C.
July 2012

# ACKNOWLEDGMENTS

Many people helped my father as he researched this book, and I don't know all of their names. For the people I inadvertently omit, I'm sorry—I came late to this process. To Steve Hammond and the staff at Congressional Cemetery; Kim Bernard Holien at Fort McNair; and Juanita Leisch of the Society for Women and the Civil War, thank you for being "early adopters" of this project. Your advice, guidance and support were so helpful to both my dad and me.

Many, many librarians need to be acknowledged at such places as the National Archives; the Washington, D.C. Public Library (especially the Washingtoniana division); and the Library of Congress. Thank you for your efficient and timely response with any and every request. Thanks to Jim Kansier, for taking the time to share his expertise on fire. To my dad's siblings, Bill Bergin, Pat Gentleman and Colleen Bergin, for cheering on this book. To Dad's family and friends, too numerous to name, who supported him in writing the book and encouraged me to get it published. To Uncle Bill Collins, for his calming help with the images for this book. To Ellen Hamilton at Yellow Dot Designs, who stepped into the breach. And to Pam Clark, who lent a hand, too.

Thank you to Jodie Allen, MaryAnn East and Mark Riddell, for having the right information at the right time and sharing it with me. And to Rachel Cummings, who said, "Hey, I want to help you get your dad's book published!" in much the same way she used to say, "Hey, let's put on a play!" To Janet Kiel, who saw the bigger picture when I did not. To Carol Francis, who was home when I called. To Michael Fritsch, who took the time to contact me and share his family's story and for his example of laboring to

ACKNOWLEDGMENTS

obtain a worthy goal. To Jim Percoco, for his guidance on how to publish a book and his advice to persevere to find the right publisher. To Hannah Cassilly from The History Press, who believed in this book from reading the proposal. To the staff at The History Press who made the book a reality.

And thank you to my husband, Mark, who knew the importance of this book to both Dad and me, and to my children, who always loved Grandpa's stories. Now here's one you can hold in your hands.

# INTRODUCTION

My dad loved to read about history, but not just "in passing." His historical reading was intense. The table next to his reading chair always held a dictionary, a notepad where he could write down quotes or questions he wanted to research further and, in case he needed to do some fact-checking, reference material on the subject he was currently pursuing. Reading, for me, is generally an escape, and even as a young child I remember sighing heavily when I would ask him what a word meant and he would point toward the dictionary, causing me to "interrupt" my reading for the pursuit of knowledge.

Thinking back, I am not sure where my dad first found out about the Arsenal explosion. A small blurb in one of the many newspapers or journals that he read, I imagine. I think he had read about Congressional Cemetery's monument to the women killed in the Arsenal explosion and went to see it. He was retired—a Civil War buff—and he was always heading out to look at a memorial, a battlefield or an exhibit of photos. I remember him talking about this explosion and the tragic loss of life, and he was surprised at how little information was available so he could learn more.

I remember noticing how in almost every conversation with him during that time—in person or on the phone—the Arsenal explosion came up. I am sure at some point during those phone conversations I rolled my eyes when he again brought up this explosion that had happened so long ago.

When he ordered the replica of a munitions trunk that the Arsenal workers used to hold the cartridges they made, I began to take more of an interest. I think that was the week he called to tell me he had re-created the process the women had to go through to fill the cartridges. It seems like some ball bearings and black pepper were key props in his reenactment.

Soon after that, he said he was going to write something about the Arsenal explosion—he just wasn't sure if there would be enough information for an article or a book. It was a mystery to him why this book had not yet been written because the story was so captivating. Many of the women working at the Arsenal that day had lost a husband or a father in the Civil War and were working to help support their families. Then there was the careless boss, the tragic explosion and, finally, a working-class community that united to erect a fitting monument to those lost lives, despite the financial cost. All with the backdrop of one of our nation's most stressful times.

Dad spent a lot of time poring through archives, census data and old photographs. He interviewed cemetery docents and museum curators. He talked with a fire marshal in order to understand how the explosion ripped through the building. As he was finishing the book, he hoped to find a descendant of someone who had been in the explosion. He put ads in Civil War magazines and on the Internet. He used the phone book and called people with the same last name as victims of the fire. He never found anyone to give a family account of the event.

My dad died unexpectedly in July 2009. He had finished his book, sent one proposal to a publisher and went on a camping trip. While on this trip, he had

Plaque commemorating the Arsenal explosion in front of George C. Marshall Hall, National Defense University, Fort McNair, Washington, D.C. *Photo by Brian Bergin.*

a heart attack. In the days and months after his funeral, many people asked me about his book and about getting it published. I set the publishing project aside many times, discouraged by the rejection letters I received. During one of those times, I received a message from Michael Fritsch, praising my dad's work, sharing how sorry he was to learn of my dad's passing and how much this research had helped him find more information about his relative who had adopted Kate Brosnahan's two children after the Arsenal explosion. At last, we had a personal account. You will find Mr. Fritsch's family story in the epilogue of this book. That contact spurred one final push for publication. This story of the hardworking souls who perished and the committed people left behind needed to be told. It was a happy day when The History Press called to say it would publish this book.

So here it is, in your hands. I am happy that you are reading it. My dad admired the hardworking immigrants from "the Island" neighborhood in Washington, D.C. He admired the community that, despite its poverty, dedicated itself to honoring the Arsenal victims. Now it's our turn to honor those long gone and keep their story alive. And it is a chance to keep a bit of my dad alive—a man who loved history and who found a little-known Civil War story and dedicated himself to making it well known.

Erin Bergin Voorheis
Leesburg, Virginia
July 13, 2012

# 1
# PRELUDE

## "AN ESPECIAL CALAMITY..."

*The saddest funeral procession that has passed along Pennsylvania Avenue since the beginning of the war traversed that great thoroughfare yesterday afternoon. We have had hundreds of these mournful manifestations in token of the valor of the brave men who have fallen in this fight for freedom, and they have become so common as to make death familiar, and to cheapen the value of human life. It would seem as if Providence had ordained that, in this struggle for the existence of a great nation, indifference to disaster and indifference to death should become a national characteristic, and that, in the pursuit of the one great object, little opportunity should be left for grief, and no time for despair.*

*But there was a memorable exception yesterday afternoon. Seventeen lovely young women, suddenly summoned into the presence of their God, without a moment's notice, by an almost inexcusable catastrophe, were followed to their graves by thousands of people. This event stands out from the honorable mortality of war as an especial calamity. These poor girls died stainlessly, in the midst of youth and beauty; died in their efforts to maintain themselves and their parent; died with the June flowers perfuming the air; died doubtless, while they were laughing over the events of the day before, and discussing the events of the coming morrow.*
—Daily Morning Chronicle, *Washington, D.C., June 20, 1864*

What follows is the long-forgotten, Civil War–era story of how twenty-one young women—the seventeen noted above, plus four other co-workers—needlessly suffered horrible, fiery deaths as the result of one man's "culpably careless" act. In referencing the culture of death that permeated civilian communities such as Washington, D.C., in the last year of the Civil War, this story explains why a community, all but inured to death and funereal trappings by the wrath of a long and terrible war, turned out to mourn and grieve in numbers not seen before and not equaled again until President Lincoln was carried from the city some ten months hence. It also acknowledges the compassionate public gesture of that war-weary and grief-burdened president whose absence from these somber events would have been neither resented, nor noted, by a public that knew well the crushing demands that could legitimately keep him behind his desk in the White House.

This is also the story of how the city's laboring class worked and sacrificed to ensure that the memory of these misfortunate women would be remembered and respected for generations after the aged survivors, rescuers and bystanders had retold the story of the "great Arsenal explosion of '64" to their grandchildren for the last time.

And while this is a story of memory, it is, at base, an account of death in a time when the mantle of death cloaked the hearths of homesites across the country. Deep-seated grief and black-hued mourning was an American motif then as common as a horse-drawn carriage or a hoop-skirted woman. Over 600,000 men would die from the effects of a war that would breathe new life into a flawed national constitution. Their exploits would, rightly, long be remembered, retold and revered. Too quickly forgotten, quite unfairly, were the deaths of others—mostly women and children—who were victims of that same conflagration and who also had stories worth remembering, retelling and revering. This account is just one of those.

To appreciate the Arsenal tragedy, as did the people of 1864 Washington, D.C., it is important to understand that this calamity came to them at a time when their reservoir of grief was close to being tapped out. The war was midway through its fourth year and, while Union victories had been many, the decisive Union victory still seemed depressingly elusive. Union losses had been substantial, and any hopes that they might decrease seemed illusionary. A depressing substantiation was even then, in the sweltering late spring of 1864, being provided in the piney forests and open pastures near a seceded Virginia village with the mystifying name of Cold Harbor.

## THE WILDERNESS CAMPAIGN AT COLD HARBOR, VIRGINIA

"I have always regretted that the last assault at Cold Harbor was ever made." A deathbed confession was long held as gospel truth in the nineteenth century, and although Ulysses S. Grant was not on his deathbed when he wrote these words, he was at death's door. Within two weeks of completing his insightful Civil War memoir in July 1885, Grant, pain-wracked with throat cancer, was dead. But back in the hot summer of 1864, "Sam" Grant was not alone in regretting the Union's version of Pickett's charge.

On the evening of May 3, 1864, Grant put in motion his configuration of the previously poorly utilized Army of the Potomac. Over the next eleven months, he would maneuver this cumbersome, blue-coated cudgel to pound Robert E. Lee's Army of Northern Virginia senseless and force it into submission. However, before a surrender could be signed at Appomattox, in

General U.S. Grant at Cold Harbor, Virginia. *Courtesy of the Library of Congress.*

April 1865 a malevolent providence required a ten-month, stalemated siege of Lee's army in the south-central Virginia transportation hub of Petersburg. This siege stood in marked contrast to the bloody and incessant fighting that preceded it through 1864's early summer months, from the banks of the Rapidan to the shores of the James. Littering its crimson wake was a flotsam of carnage so great that only by comparison to the slaughter at Cold Harbor were the tolls of the Wilderness, Spotsylvania and North Anna allocated to the ranks of secondary interest. For the general public, however, these bloated ranks of dead, wounded and missing were sorrows not yet fully known.

On May 13, the fog of ignorance would allow correspondent Noah Brooks to spout optimism, as he wrote in his diary:

> *Every loyal heart is full of joy at the glorious tidings which continue to come up from the front; and citizens everywhere are congratulating each other*

*upon the near prospect of an end of this wasteful and wicked war. The "coming man" appears to have come at last, and Grant is the hero of the war. His name is on every lip in praise, and his wonderful persistence, his determined courage, and masterly skill all justify the fondest expectations of his friends and the hopes of all who love their country and trust in Grant. It really does seem that God has suffered the hour of our bitter trial and adversity to pass away.*

Prescient in his description of Grant as the "coming man" and accurate, at the time, in reporting the name of Grant on praiseful lips, neither Brooks nor the Northern public was prepared for the harsh and bloody demonstration that would deprive them of the illusion that their "hour of bitter trial and adversity" would soon pass.

In the period from May 5 to June 12, Grant reported losses of more than thirty-nine thousand soldiers. Over time, the historical abacus would calculate the figure closer to fifty thousand. However, neither the accounting methods of the day nor the sensitivities of political reality allowed for a timely, let alone accurate, accounting of battlefield casualties. Sensitive to their potential for inducing despair in the public and fostering discord in the soon-to-begin National Unity Party[1] presidential nominating convention, Secretary of War Edwin M. Stanton released Grant's casualty figures in drips and drabs, as if he were rationing allocations of grief and sorrow.

For the citizens of Washington, the first evidence that Grant's final triumph would not be cause for an especially festive Fourth of July that year was not the newspaper accounts of lengthy casualty lists but the more direct experience of the disturbing sights and disconcerting sounds of many hundreds of Grant's wounded being off-loaded from river steamers at the Capital's Sixth Street wharf, on the eastern bank of the Potomac River. Regardless of the exact numbers, the gruesome cargo continuously discharged from the decks and holds of a motley fleet of improvised water ambulances made it alarmingly clear to Washingtonians that something had, once again, gone seriously wrong on the road to a quick and blood-sparse victory.

By May 28, Brooks's tone had markedly changed as he reported that the

*night before last 3,000 severely wounded men were landed at the Sixth Street wharf; and the sight will not soon be forgotten by those who witnessed it. The long, ghastly procession of shattered wrecks; the groups of fearful, sympathetic spectators; the rigid shapes of those who are bulletioned as "since dead"; the smoothly flowing river and the solemn hush in foreground and on distant evening shores—all form a picture which must some day perpetuate for the nation the saddest sight of all this war—"The return of the wounded." Many women and even men weep from sympathy and cannot see the silent suffering of these wounded braves unmoved.*

The capital, in Brooks's diary, had become "a great hospital." If so, the wards of that great hospital were twenty-one white-framed medical facilities spread throughout the District and its suburbs, and "every one of them…full of the wounded and dying…"

Although there are no accounts of President Lincoln watching the Wilderness Campaign wounded being unloaded at the Sixth Street wharf, subsequent comments and actions clearly indicated that three years of bloody fighting had not hardened his gentle heart to the sufferings of either his soldiers or his citizens.

When Grant agreed to assume command of all the Union armies, Lincoln had promised to let him lead as he saw best. The president, in contrast to past practice, would not meddle in strategy or tactics and would not second-

President Lincoln with son Tad in 1864. *Courtesy of the Library of Congress.*

guess his fighting general. But "meddling" was in the eye of the president. Having convinced himself that a visit to the front was not what he meant by meddling, Lincoln arranged for a costal steamer to take him, and his son Tad, to Grant's headquarters at City Point, Virginia.

With that promise not to meddle still operative in his mind, if not in his actions, Lincoln, nonetheless, needed to assure himself that the staggering death toll of the last six weeks was the bondsman's just price for the elimination of die-hard Confederate resistance, rather than Union generalship, once again, gone amuck.

But first, he had to go to Philadelphia, where his words would make clear that the blood-soaked tally weighed heavy on his mind. A few days later, back home in Washington, his actions would dramatically demonstrate to a grief-laden city that the reservoir of tenderness in his war-torn heart was not yet exhausted.

# PHILADELPHIA—THURSDAY, JUNE 16, 1864

It was 6:30 a.m., and President Lincoln was already at the B&O train station a few blocks north of Capitol Hill, just ahead of the murderous heat that brutalized the usually more pleasant nature of Washington's Junes. With Mrs. Lincoln, and an entourage of Pennsylvania politicians, the president was journeying to Philadelphia for the Great Central Sanitary Fair. The "Great Fair" was a fundraising extravaganza for the voluntary Sanitary and Christian Commission that provided the Union army with much of its battlefield medical services. Although the North had hoped that Grant would make short work of Lee's vaunted Army of Northern Virginia, the ever-lengthening, and increasingly blood-soaked, roster of Union casualties from the Wilderness Campaign indicated that the war's end was not yet in reach. The services of the Sanitary Commission, it appeared, would be needed indefinitely. So, despite the enthusiastic track-side receptions Lincoln received as the train chugged its way east and north past stations in Baltimore, Havre de Grace, Newark, Wilmington and Chester, it was the casualty lists that darkly dominated Lincoln's thoughts as he finished writing the brief set of remarks he would make that night at dinner.

In Philadelphia, with the four-and-a-half-hour rail trip and a tour of the fair behind him, Lincoln was ushered to dinner in a nearby supper room. In response to an introduction disguised as a dinner table toast, Lincoln rose to address an enthusiastic audience. Interspersed among the starch-collared political elites and rank and file ward workers waiting to hear the president speak were notables such as Edward Everett, the featured speaker at last November's dedication of the Gettysburg Cemetery, and General Lew Wallace, who in a few weeks would delay Confederate general Jubal Early's advance on Washington and would, years later, write the biblical epic we know as *Ben Hur*.

President Lincoln in 1864. *Courtesy of the Library of Congress.*

Lincoln, burdened with the nightmare of some fifty thousand Union casualties from Grant's month-long campaign against Lee, began his talk with a dark introduction: "War, at best, is terrible, and this of ours, in its magnitude and duration, is one of the most terrible the world has ever known." After iterating some of the conflict's deleterious effects, he went on to say, "It has carried mourning among us until the heavens may be said to be hung in black." As if the mournful weight of these words were not enough, he added, "And yet it continues." There were more words of explanation, description and exhortation, followed by wild applause and the presentation of a silver medal from the ladies of Philadelphia. There would be more toasts and more touring before the night was over. Throughout, the receptions were friendly and the crowds welcoming, despite the fact that Lincoln's comments had given a mournfully thought-provoking tone to the evening. And although his words were intended to be encouragingly supportive, hindsight allows us to see them as morbidly prophetic.

Returning to Washington at about twelve-thirty the next afternoon, June 17, 1864, his arrival was greeted by a menacing black cloud of smoke, billowing high into the midday sky from the city's southern edge. Even without an explanation, it would have been clear to the burdened president that something devastatingly untoward had befallen the Washington Arsenal in the District's poor "Island" neighborhood. The record is blank as to whom it was who first advised the president about the disaster, but Lincoln must have seen that due to this terrible event, the heavens were, actually, hung in black.

## The Island: A Hardscrabble, Tenderhearted Washington Neighborhood

Although it was called "the Island," none ever mistook it for a paradise. It was one of the oldest residential communities in Washington and, on a Civil War–era map, was readily identifiable as it hung from the city's center like a geographic appendix. Its western border was the Potomac River, while its south shores, once known as Greenleaf's Point, were buffeted by the Anacostia River, then called the Eastern Branch. Much of its northern portal was edged by a truncated version of The Mall, hosting an incomplete Washington Monument, the Smithsonian's brownstone castle, an armory and hundreds of bivouacked Union troops. A sense of island isolation was induced by the Washington Canal, which opened from the Potomac on the west and then paralleled the northern edge of The Mall for three-quarters of a mile, along what is now Constitution Avenue. It then dropped south to cut its way through the city's southeast landmass to the Eastern Branch in a series of increasingly steep stair steps. The community, clearly delimited to the south and west of the canal, came to be called the Island.

An additional locator aid was the "Long Bridge," which stretched like a schoolmarm's birch pointer diagonally across the Potomac from the Virginia shore, just north of Alexandria, to Maryland Avenue, a heavily used, unpaved city thoroughfare that funneled travelers, troops and trains through the top of the Island to the Capitol's central commercial district at the foot of Capitol Hill. Boats of all types, be they steam or sail, civilian or military, cargo or touring, docked at the bustling wharves whose wooden docks and profitable warehouses terminated both Sixth and Seventh Streets. There the Island's stevedores traded the outgoing tools and supplies of war for incoming racks of lumber, hogsheads of Pennsylvania whiskey and the bloodied bodies of wounded Union soldiers. The transfers, whether commercial or humanitarian, were incessant and interrupted neither by holidays nor by nighttime shadows.

Portions of the Island had a rural character with a windmill and dirt roads that cut through wide-open, undeveloped tracts of farmland—mostly in its western acres—that lone travelers and unarmed soldiers wisely avoided after dark.

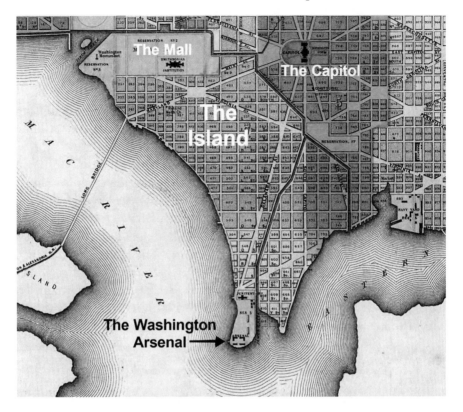

The Island neighborhood, Washington, D.C. *From* Johnson's Georgetown and the City of Washington *by Johnson and Ward (New York: Johnson and Ward, 1862). Courtesy of the U.S. Historical Archive.*

Its more densely packed areas, such as those that bordered The Mall, housed a thriving red-light district whose "resorts" handled the overflow from the pricey brothels and two-bit whorehouses that inundated Pennsylvania Avenue in an area derisively called "Hooker's Division." In her 1941 book, *Reveille in Washington: 1860–1865*, Margaret Leech reported on the antics of an Island family named Light. Ms. Leech wrote that "there were five Lights: father, mother, and three daughters; and they had made themselves notorious in every unsavory section of the capital…Noisy, quarrelsome and outrageously profane, the sisters were repeatedly sent to the workhouse…In the autumn, they were back on the Island, incorrigibly open for business in new quarters in Pear Tree Alley."

The Island was also known as the home of Washington's federal arsenal. A spacious industrial campus and military encampment, established in 1791, it occupied several hundred acres in the Island's extreme southwest quadrant.

A hulking brick structure, once the District's penitentiary, dominated the northern portion of the compound. In 1862, however, that facility was taken over by the Ordnance Department, and its cells and hallways were filled with military equipment and ammunition rather than assorted types of felons and convicts. Later, in the aftermath of President Lincoln's assassination, the conspirators would be held, tried and executed behind its walls and the body of John Wilkes Booth temporarily buried in its cellar.

The Arsenal compound housed over forty permanent brick or frame structures devoted to the production of death-dealing materiel. Within its confines could be found facilities, called "laboratories" or "manufactories," producing ammunitions for field artillery, muskets, carbines and handguns, as well as flares and rockets. In support of its deadly raison d'être were powder magazines, icehouses, carpentry and paint shops, toolsheds, stables and storage yards. There was a blacksmith shop, a bakery, a hospital, a commissary and quarters for both officers and enlisted ranks, as well as housing for married men. Lumber, leather and gunpowder moved into and boxes of artillery

The North Front of the Washington Arsenal. *Courtesy of the Library of Congress.*

shells, rocket flares, cartridges and percussion caps moved out of the Arsenal via a system of rail lines, wagon roads and riverside wharves. The Arsenal had a fleet of 56 wagons that were kept busy throughout the day, and often well into the night, hauling material one way or the other. During one survey, 128 wagons passed through the Arsenal's front gate in a period of one and a half hours. In March 1862, it was reported that the Arsenal's magazines were packed with 16,500,000 rounds of small-arms ammunition.

Although its open spaces were filled mostly with artillery carriages, ammunition limbers and waist-high pyramids of cannon shot, the grounds were nonetheless green and arbor-like and, at least in its northern sector, fit for a Sunday picnic or a cool evening's stroll.

Legend has it that shortly after moving into the White House, an insatiable curiosity and an unidentifiable sound in the night led President Lincoln out of the Executive Mansion, across The Mall, down through the Island and to the gates of the Arsenal, which he found open and unguarded. Once the security breech was corrected, stories persisted that he would, on occasion, seek a break from the tensions of the presidency through night strolls around the river breeze–cooled Arsenal grounds.

Although once dominated by rural pastureland, the Arsenal had changed the Island's character from bucolic to industrial, and the demands of the war intensified the shift from laconic to bustling. These changes were dramatized by the intense development of the Island's residential sections. Pierre Charles L'Enfant, hired to plan Washington's streets, created an overlay of ridged, right-angled intersecting streets, with numbered streets running north to south and alphabet-lettered streets going east and west. It was an efficient design, compromised by the state-named grand avenues that played havoc with horse-and-buggy traffic by slicing through the grid at inconvenient angles. This system of streets and avenues created dramatic vistas for monuments and memorials and also provided a framework for the labyrinth of shacks, shanties and clapboarded rooming houses that were home to Washington's hard-strapped mechanics, laborers, teamsters and prostitutes. Neither sewers nor sidewalks serviced the Island's warrens of dusty streets and dank allies. Its appeal lay not in its aesthetics but in its low rents and walkable proximity to the jobs available in the places like the Arsenal, on the riverside wharfs to the west, in the massive Navy Yard just to the east of the Island, in the Central Market area to the north and on the nearby unfinished Capitol Building.

The Island's main portal was 4½ Street, which, on a Civil War–era map, runs plumb straight from Pennsylvania Avenue down to the Arsenal's entrance at T Street. That same map shows the Island's geographic center as being around the intersection of 4½ and K Streets South.

Packed into the Island's ramshackle and run-down residences were thousands of working families of low and moderate means. Edward Adams, a huckster at the City's Center Market, lived with his thirty-six-year-old wife, Nancy, and their seven children—ranging from sixteen years old to one year—on Seventh Street between G and H Streets. Thaddeus Brahler, a forty-eight-year-old tailor from Germany, lived with his wife and six children on E Street, between 4½ and 6th Streets. Samuel Collins, a forty-two-year-old laborer; his wife, Catherine; and their three children lived immediately adjacent to the Arsenal's entrance on 4½ Street. Mrs. Ann Arnold, a forty-one-year-old widow working as a dressmaker, lived with her two young daughters in a house on the corner of 4½ and G Streets. Similar families, some bigger and others smaller, a few richer and many poorer, new immigrants and native born, free black and low-paid white, were to be found residing in unhealthful proximity across the Island.

Serving the Islanders' spiritual needs were at least ten Christian churches within the Island's confines. In 1864, Methodists, the nation's largest denomination, would have dominated the city's churchgoing populations. However, internal divisions over the issue of slavery had torn the church apart in 1844, and a new composite, the Methodist-Episcopal church, emerged in the wake of the schism. The Island's diverse inventory of churches included: to the west, at the corner of Tenth and D Streets, the Ryland Methodist Chapel; farther east on Seventh between D and E Streets, the Seventh Street Presbyterian Church, and to the south on L Street, the Gorsuch Methodist Episcopal Chapel; and in the northern sector on F between Sixth and Seventh, serving the Island's Irish Catholic population, St. Dominick's. Also represented were Baptists, Episcopals, Calvinists and a lone "colored" church. In addition to a number of other churches in nearby neighborhoods, there was also an active Temperance Hall for those who supported this religious-like movement's mission to banish the evil effects of alcohol from the family circle, in particular, and social life in general. Many Island residents were to be found on the membership rolls of these off-Island congregations.

Even though the community was poor and its people hard-pressed, they were not indifferent to the suffering inflicted by the war that raged in the farm fields and along the country byways just across the Potomac. A telling example of the Island's tender side occurred in the early days of the fighting, as the Union army struggled to develop an effective system to deal with its battlefield casualties. Near the end of June 1862, a night train brought several hundred casualties from a battle at Front Royal, Virginia, to the Maryland Avenue depot at the Island's end of the Long Bridge. Communication breakdowns confused the transportation coordination that would ordinarily characterize such an operation. The result was that the railcars, with their cargo of wounded and dying, were sidetracked and then left unattended because the overworked military doctor went home to sleep when no medical staff or ambulances arrived to manage the transfer to hospitals. Alerted to the suffering of the abandoned soldiers by the Island's back-fence telegraph, residents soon converged on the rail depot and took matters into their own hands.

The wounded were given water and fresh bandages and carried from the stifling confines of the railcars to the pews of nearby churches and the benches of accessible assembly halls. Throughout the night, Island residents did their limited best to comfort the soldiers' suffering until military authorities were again able to assume control the next morning. Although never repeated on such a massive scale, the army's incompetence would give the Islanders' kindness ample opportunity to display itself during the years of war that followed.

## THE NATION'S CAPITAL: "A NOTORIOUSLY FILTHY CITY"

As hard as life may have been for the Island's saints, sinners, soldiers and shysters, many parts of the capital city were only marginally better. Of the few things shared by both rich and poor, one was the inescapable squalor of public life in Washington. With the exception of portions of Pennsylvania Avenue, the capital's streets were unpaved, subjecting the poor, the proletariat and the prosperous to throat-choking dust in the hot summers, shoe-top-deep mud after the spring's rains and ankle-twisting ruts the rest of the year. With the passing of winter, the thaw of frost lifted and loosened the few cobblestone walkways bordering Pennsylvania Avenue to such an extent that schemers and scofflaws easily stole the sidewalks right out from under the city's muddy feet.

Public sanitation was appalling. Outhouses, latrines, chamber pots and darkened alleys served as lavatories. While horses and mules may have been the backbone of commerce and quartermasters, their droppings littered the public thoroughfares and made a street crossing by hoop-skirted ladies and high-booted gentlemen an exercise in attention and agility.

In the days before the existence of the Humane Society, beasts of burden were regularly worked to death on the capital's streets and their carcasses left to molder where they fell. The District's public street sanitarians, whose job it was to remove festering health hazards, were regularly slow to react, haphazard in their patrolling and careless with sanitizing protocols, such as they were.

Packs of dogs ran wild throughout the city, spreading rabies, attacking pedestrians, panicking horses and generally terrorizing citizens. Police officers were issued rifles and authorized to shoot mad dogs, roaming mongrels and flea-bitten strays.

The canal bordering the Island and bisecting the city, having long ago ceased functioning as an artery of commerce, now served the butchers and vegetable merchants of the Central Market, the dysentery-racked soldiers encamped along its banks and the nocturnal crimes of the city's thugs and brigands as a convenient depository and open sewer.

Flies, fleas and cockroaches were as thick in summertime Washington as were the mosquitoes and methane vapors emanating from the nearby swampy morass called Foggy Bottom.

The city, with its theaters and churches, parks and parlors, afternoon teas and evening balls, had unique charm to offer its privileged and pedigreed. But these enjoyments came with a price that was often odorous, offensive, dirty and uncomfortable. For the poor and the working class, however, the city's entertainments, at least those outside the family, were few, while its discomforts were all too near and nagging.

2

# FRIDAY, JUNE 17, 1864

## THE ARSENAL'S PYROTECHNIST

Although it was early, Tom Brown was already at work and busy, inadvertently, setting in place the elements preliminary to, but essential for, Washington's worst Civil War disaster. For twenty-three years, forty-seven-year-old Thomas Brown had worked as a "pyrotechnist" at the Arsenal and now was its superintendent. He was an Islander and lived with his wife and two teenage daughters on 4½ Street between M and N—a respectable section peopled with brick-makers, boat builders, prison guards and blacksmiths within walking distance of the Arsenal.

His job was to oversee the production of the various explosive powders and devices manufactured there for use by the U.S. military in its sidearms, muskets, carbines, field artillery and rockets. Mr. Brown worked from a formula book that the army chief of ordnance distributed to all its arsenals. Familiarity with the basics, and years of experience with the results, gave Brown the confidence—if not the authority—to alter the fireworks recipes in the name of a better product.

This morning's task was the final step in the production of a new batch of red and white flares, referred to as "stars." Every year at about this time, Brown's flare inventory dropped noticeably as Union field commanders ordered additional cases of reds and whites, not in anticipation of increased night attacks by Confederate cavalry but in hopes of celebrating an old-fashioned Yankee Fourth of July holiday. In the 1861 split between North and South, Independence Day was a celebration that the North celebrated and the Rebels shunned. Just a year prior, in 1863, for example, Confederate

Modern-day pyrotechnic "star" flares. *Courtesy of Harry Gilliam, Skylighter Fireworks Company.*

general John Pemberton had delayed surrendering Vicksburg to General Grant for twenty-four hours in the hope that a surrender on the Fourth of July would bring the Confederates better terms. It did not.

This morning, Brown was one of the few Washingtonians pleased with the oppressive heat wave that brought starch-wilting August temperatures to the capital in mid-June. A popular daily feature of the *Evening Star* newspaper titled "State of the Thermometer" reported the previous day's high temperature as registered at the Franklin & Co. Opticians' outdoor thermometer on Pennsylvania Avenue. Since the start of June, midday temperatures in the nineties had been common, and three-digit reports were discomfortingly frequent.

Superintendent Brown, uncomfortable in the heat just as much as everybody else, was nonetheless pleased because the high temperatures would quicken the drying time needed for his latest batch of stars. The wet flare mixture of exactly weighted portions of potassium chloride (chlorate of potash), strontium nitrate (nitrate of strontin) and copul (carbon) was formed into gumball-sized pellets, placed one deep on the bottom of black-

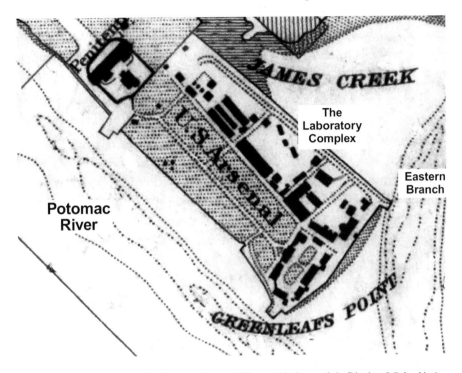

An annotated map of the Washington Arsenal. *Topographical map of the District of Columbia/ surveyed in the year '59 by A. Boschke; engraved by D. McClelland, Washington, D.C. Courtesy of the U.S. Historical Archive.*

painted copper pans and set outside for several days to dry and harden. Today, Brown's focus was on three large, round pans, each filled with two to three hundred damp pellets. By 8:00 a.m., with pans in tow, he was on his way to his favorite drying site.

A service road, fringed by a white picket fence, ran east to west across the lower end of the center third of the Arsenal grounds. A couple of large storehouses and a carpenter's shop occupied the west side of the road, while a forge, a small storehouse and the post bakery were on the north side. Taking up most of the remaining space was a small arms repair facility, a few miscellaneous support buildings and a rambling storage yard. A wedge-shaped sliver of land to the east contained a north–south service road and a compact cluster of laboratory buildings. It was here, in an out-of-the-way spot on the ground between a small magazine and the south side of the cartridge-making shop that Brown chose to dry his new batch of stars. He had used this location for years, liking it because it was convenient to most of the munitions facilities running along the eastern edge of the campus.

Appealing too was the fact that the threat of some inattentive laborer or roaming equine accidentally overturning his hard-wrought stars was minimal since few of either had cause to tramp through an isolated byway obstructed by piles of board lumber.

# THE LABORATORY

The Laboratory, at the center of the Arsenal grounds near its eastern edge, along a swampy wetland euphemistically named James Creek, was actually a cluster of three buildings.

The largest, built as the original laboratory in 1844, was the first in the laboratory complex and the one below which lay the drying fireworks. It was a five-room, one-story wooden rectangular structure whose long back wall was made of brick.

Its front opened on the service road edging the Arsenal's eastern flank. Although built as the original laboratory, it had at some point been converted to a storehouse and only recently refitted as a multifunctional ordnance facility.

View of the Washington Arsenal facility. *Courtesy of the U.S. National Archives.*

A covered loading dock dominated the center half of the building and connected the north and south wings of the unit. The dock also provided access to the interior work areas through a large freight door that received lumber and supplies and shipped filled ammunition boxes over to the Arsenal's magazines. At either end of the dock were access doors, designed as entry and exit points for cargo-laden hand trucks, and the laboratory's workers, messengers and infrequent visitors.

Directly behind the east-facing freight door was the Box Room, where wagonloads of White Pine boards were received and, with the skills of apprentice-level carpenters and the aid of simple hand tools, converted into ammunition boxes. A lidded box, approximately fifteen inches long, nine inches wide and five high, held one thousand .54-caliber cartridges for the breech-loading Sharps carbine rifle favored by the likes of Sheridan's cavalry units.

Sergeants of the Twenty-second New York State Militia lean on a stack of Washington Arsenal cartridges at Harper's Ferry, 1862. *Courtesy of Michael Murtaugh.*

Each box was painted olive, in accord with an Ordnance Department color code for the type of ammunition it held. Content information was stenciled in white on the outside. When filled, a box weighed seventy-eight pounds.

To the right of the Box Room, and occupying the northern wing of the building, was the Cylinder Room. Here specially treated sheets of paper or linen were cut and rolled into cylinders sized to exact specifications and designed to hold a precise measurement of fifty grains of gunpowder. As a safety measure, distinct tasks involving the use of gunpowder were performed in separate buildings. For this reason, the empty cylinders were taken from the Cylinder Room and carried to the Filling Room, located in another laboratory building just south of the Choking and Packing Building. There, "chargers"—wood, brass or copper tubes holding a precise allocation of gunpowder—were used to fill each cylinder with the precise amount of powder needed to make a lead bullet lethal to any Confederate within two hundred yards of a charging trooper. As they were filled, the cylinders—still open at the top—were placed upright in pigeonholed boxes. Filled boxes were then carted back to the Choking Room. The Choking Room occupied the southern quarter of the old laboratory building. Connecting it with the Packing Room, and spanning the laboratory's office area, was a narrow oblong passageway.

"Choking" involved inserting a lead bullet into the powder-filled cylinder, tying off the bullet end of the cartridge with a couple rounds of thread and placing the closed cartridge into a workbox that sat a few feet in front of the "choker." When eventually filled, the boxes were promptly removed and replaced with empties by the Laboratory's contingent of boy porters. In that interval

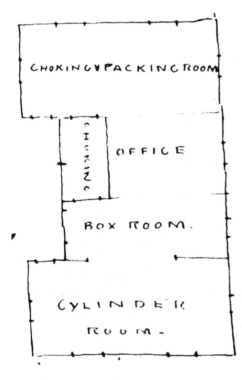

General George Ramsay's 1864 sketch of the laboratory's configuration. *Courtesy of the U.S. National Archives.*

between when the last few cartridges filled in the topmost row and the box was taken away, the workers could not be blamed if, only for an instant, they believed they shared the same threat as a frontline soldier facing a rank of one thousand steely-eyed Georgia sharpshooters. A choker's fidgeting and nervous positioning prior to again seeing the welcome gape of an empty replacement box might have helped instill a renewed sense in the mind of an apprehensive worker that this job, tedious though it may be, was not as dangerous as rumor had it. If such were his thoughts, time and fate would soon prove them absolutely wrong.

The safety section of the Ordnance Department Operating Manual required that only the minimum amount of powder and ammunition be on hand at any one time. Specifically, the manual cautioned, "Never keep in the laboratory more powder than is necessary, and have the ammunition… taken to the magazine as fast as it is finished." In a procedure inconsistent with this wise precaution, filled cartridge boxes were not removed from the building but rather were simply carried to the other side of the room where the packing operation was located.

Packing was a two-step process. First, the choked cartridges were wrapped in a waterproof paper bundle of ten. Each bundle also contained the supply of a dozen percussion caps that a trooper would need to fire the cartridges. Next, the cartridge bundles were tightly packed into newly constructed ammunition boxes lined with waterproof paper. A thousand-round ammunition box contained a single row of packets lying five high, running along one side of the box. To minimize spillage, the remainder of the space was snugged up with cartridge bundles placed vertically on end.[2]

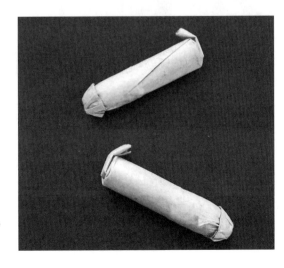

An example of a .54 cartridge, similar to the ones the Arsenal women were choking on June 17, 1864. *Courtesy of Stephen Burgess, Campsite Artifacts.*

With the addition of a wooden lid, screwed securely in place, and a coating of water repellant, the assembly job was completed. At this point, the sealed boxes were removed from the laboratory and stored in one of the Arsenal's magazines until needed in the field. With an experienced staff engaged for ten of the twelve-hour shift, the Washington Arsenal turned out over twenty-one thousand cartridges a day in the spring of 1864.[3]

Mr. Brown oversaw the work of the laboratory with the help of his young assistant, Andrew Cox, the Arsenal's chief clerk, twenty-one-year-old Hosea Moulton—a thrice-wounded and highly decorated Union veteran—and Major E.N. Stebbins, the Arsenal's storekeeper. Their office, not so much a distinct room as an identifiable space, was awkwardly located in the center of the laboratory, directly behind the narrow corridor connecting the Choking and Box Rooms. While a wall separated the office from the corridor, only the nature of the work and the space-filling bulk of miscellaneous ordnance supplies divided the office from the Choking and Packing Room to the south and the Box Room to the north. The only way in or out of the office was through one or the other of the shop-floor work areas. Whether by design or oversight, the effect was that the workers were subject to constant observation by one of the four supervisory staff.

A cadre of 110 women did the laboratory's production work. Eighty were engaged in making the cylinders, constructing the wooden boxes or packing battle-ready cartridges into ammunition boxes. Filling an area along the south wall was the choking staff, consisting of thirty women. These tasks tended to border just beyond the space claimed by the office in the center portion of the

Boy Sweepers at the Washington Arsenal. *The Washington Arsenal Manufactory Women Killed in the Explosion, (circa 1864). Courtesy of the National Archives and Records Administration, College Park, Maryland, Still Photo Division.*

building. There were also three boys whose job it was to replace full boxes with empties, sweep sawdust and gunpowder off the carpeted floor, run messages and generally do what was asked of them by their supervisors. In contrast to the women, whose routines restricted them to the area defined by their work, the boys could be found moving about the building and, indeed, the Arsenal's grounds, if they could be found at all on a summer's day.

# WORKING WOMEN

The makeup of the laboratory's staff partly reflected the condition of wartime in the capital's labor market. With many Washington men off fighting for one side or the other, women were filling the District's understaffed desks, benches and nursing wards. The early stages of this transition from male to female workers were, however, daunting, degrading and, in some respects, dangerous.

By the start of the Civil War, women were well established in the framework of some workplaces, particularly industry. Estimates are that 25 percent of the nation's manufacturing work was done by women, with that proportion reaching over 60 percent in the mills of New England. In contrast, anyone having business in an office of federal, state or local government, a bank, a retail store or even a classroom was more likely to deal with a Tom, Dick or Harry than a Sally, Sue or Miss Emma. The emptying of offices and schoolhouses in response to the nation's call to arms, coupled with expanding opportunities in servicing a voracious war economy, created demands for which women were the chief recourse. Seeing the employment demand, and feeling the pinch of economic need, women were quick to respond.

In 1861, Dorothea Dix, a Massachusetts matron widely respected for her labors with, and on behalf of, the poor, was appointed superintendent of women nurses for the Union army. Despite the fact that she would need all the capable women she could muster to comfort the tide of wounded that would pass into her care, Dix instituted strict hiring criteria that she personally, and vigorously, enforced. Medical skills, good intentions or simple availability were not enough. To work the halls and wards of Washington's military hospitals, thought Miss Dix, a women had to be agile enough to "turn a full-grown man around in bed," coarse enough to handle odorous cartloads of sloshing bedpans and piles of blood-soiled linens, confident enough to sacrifice the space-gobbling fashions of the hoop skirt for the more angular shapes of shirt-waisted dresses and—perhaps most importantly to her—plain

Dorothea Dix (undated). *Courtesy of the Library of Congress.*

enough to smother the ardor of young men too long away from home. Fortunately for the suffering soldier, women were up to the challenge.

At about the same time as Ms. Dix was recruiting nurses, the U.S. Treasury was justifying its pioneering practice of hiring female clerks on the grounds of necessity. Military enlistments made literate men increasingly scarce, while local women who could read and write were in abundance. As if the implications of the basic laws of supply and demand were not apparent, federal treasurer Francis Spinner defended the hiring of women on the grounds that women could be paid less to do the same work as men. Commendable as was Spinner's hiring policy—if not his reasoning—the department could have benefited from implementing its own version of Dorothea Dix's hiring practices.

In the spring of 1864, with women now well represented in Washington's myriad public offices, a scandal erupted from the still sparkling halls of the newly constructed Treasury Building next to the White House. Reacting to rumors of fraud in his realm, treasury secretary Salmon P. Chase assigned Lafayette Baker, the District's brutish provost marshal, to conduct a secret investigation of departmental personnel and their accounting practices. Whatever fiscal problems may have existed, Baker shunted them aside in favor of sensational stories of the officials' perverse hiring practices and immoral job-retention requirements for treasury women.[4] Congressman James Brooks of New York initiated an investigation under the direction of the future president, James A. Garfield. Given wider leeway and basking in greater street-side recognition, Marshal Baker intensified his efforts. His investigative skills, however, continued to miss the exploitive behavior of mid-level treasury officials and focused on the indiscretions of a few vulnerable and callow young women. Both heavy-handed and misdirected, the marshal's tactics ran amuck over the lives and reputations of many innocent women. By the time Baker was reined in and himself brought up on charges, one of his teenage targets was dead, two of her friends were imprisoned in the Old Capitol jail and the characters of all "government girls" made fodder for barroom jokes and saloon hall banter.

## NEED-BASED HIRING

In contrast to the rule for which the treasury scandal proved the exception, many qualified and capable women in wartime Washington were hired based on the influence of friends or, more admirably, on obvious and deserving economic need. And it was these characteristics, rather than sexual favors or competitive examinations, that filled the civilian employment slots at the Washington Arsenal. A number of noble examples of how this benign favoritism might have worked in practice are obvious in the backgrounds of the cartridge-making employees.

The oddly named Pinkey Scott was thirty-one years old in June 1864. Under circumstances not reported, her husband died, leaving her to support herself and two young children, Annie and Willie. As a widow with dependents, Mrs. Scott would have been welcomed to fill a vacancy in the Arsenal Laboratory ranks, particularly if she had been recommended by friends or relatives who already worked there.

Twenty-year-old Johanna Connor may have gotten her job at the Arsenal's Laboratory because her mother was widowed two years before when Johanna's father died of sunstroke while working on the Arsenal grounds. In addition, her brother-in-law, Charles Curtain, may have been employed there already as a laborer.

Twenty-three-year-old Emma Tippett, whose wounded husband was with the First Regiment of the D.C. Cavalry as it moved toward the siege of Petersburg, worked in the laboratory to supplement her husband's thirteen-dollars-per-month private's pay. An active member of the Island's Seventh Street Presbyterian Church, Emma probably prayed regularly that her meager Arsenal wages, supplemented by what her mother made as a dressmaker, would be enough to keep the two of them fed and housed until her wounded husband recovered and returned to her.

Sallie McElfresh also worked to supplement her family's income. Personable and well respected, Sallie's thirty-six-year-old father worked in a paint crew at the Navy Yard, just to the east of the Island. Since 1852, John and Eliza McElfresh had had seven children. Ten-year-old Florence was born in 1854. Phedora Linthicum, born in February 1856, lived for fourteen months and died in April 1857. Later that year, in December, a newly born McElfresh infant would die and be buried, unnamed. In June 1859, Eliza gave birth to another child, who also died unnamed. Mary, born in March 1860, died at the age of ten months in December 1860. In November 1863, Eliza, now six months pregnant, would become a widow when husband John died in a typhoid epidemic. In February 1864, Eliza gave birth to a third baby who died unnamed. Friends would help the devastated McElfresh family by getting Sallie a job in the laboratory. Sallie was twelve years old.

At twelve, Sallie McElfresh was likely the youngest of the laboratory workers. Many of her co-workers, however, were not much older. Lizzie Brahler was thirteen; Annie Bache was about seventeen; Melissa Adams and Ellen Roche were eighteen; and Emma Baird, Susie Harris and Kate (also

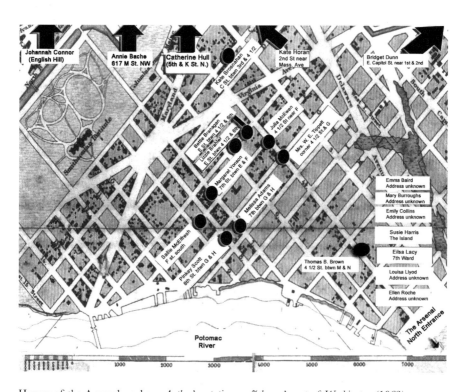

Homes of the Arsenal workers. *Author's notations on Johnson's map of Washington (1862).*

known as Catherine and Margaret) Horan were all nineteen. The thirtyish Pinkey Scott and the forty-year-old Rebecca Hull were among the oldest of the laboratory workers. Between Rebecca Hull and Sallie McElfresh were another twenty hardworking women in their twenties.

## "A Scanty Respectable Subsistence..."

If humane considerations guided the selection of which women would fill the cartridge-making employment slots, nineteenth-century production theories dictated that women, rather than men, were best able to do this vital work. The long-held assumptions of the day were that, because of smaller hands and greater dexterity, women were more efficient and better able to pack and choke the lethal cartridges. Perhaps of greater note to bureau heads and paymasters, however, was the fact that whatever the job, it was cheaper to replace men with female workers. Across the board, the pay for women was about half that for men doing the same task. The effect was that the health and well-being of a household inevitably shrank when an employed husband left for the army, a brother became disabled or a father died in his prime, even if the wife, daughter, sister or mother immediately found work. A woman laboring to support a family in wartime Washington, particularly a family without an employed male, could expect a life with significantly less of whatever had previously been taken for granted. Typically compromised were expectations for replacement clothing, balanced meals and heating comfort. And as if this catalogue of lower expectations was not disconcerting enough, the earned wages, whatever the amount, always lagged behind the dollar-warping effect of unchecked inflation. In June 1861, a shopper at the city's Center Market on Pennsylvania Avenue between Seventh and Ninth Streets could purchase a pound of beef, a dozen eggs and a peck of Irish potatoes for $0.68; in June 1864, the same purchases cost $1.35. While the wealthy might feel inconvenienced by the escalating costs, the working class and the poor were increasingly hard pressed. Estimates are that in 1863, a family of five needed $1,300 per year to get by comfortably. Few working women, and none of the Arsenal women, would ever be paid anything approaching that amount.

Although many male workers received periodic wage adjustments during the war, government wages never kept pace with those in the private sector. Masons, among the highest paid of the federal skilled trades, received $4.00 to $4.50 per day, while experienced carpenters and painters topped out at

$3.50 per day. Helpers and common laborers started at $1.75 and could receive as much as $2.25 per day. Within the same general pay range, a typical government clerk could expect to be paid $2.00 to $3.00 a day, although some made as much as $1,600 per year. Women, however, were generally the lowest-paid workers, with few receiving more than $1.10 per day and some as little as $0.40 cents. Pay rates varied among women based on experience, age and whether the worker was hired at a flat-rate-per-day or piecework scale.

Whatever the level of pay, all the Arsenal employees worked twelve-hour shifts, starting at 6:00 a.m. and ending at 6:00 p.m., six days a week. The work routine was broken with two one-hour breaks, one for breakfast and another for lunch, then commonly called dinner.

Putting the plight of workingwomen in perspective was a petition received by President Lincoln in July 1864. The petition, from "twenty thousand working women of Philadelphia" noted that even at the start of the Civil War, "the [wages] paid at the United States Arsenal...were barely sufficient to enable the women engaged upon Government work to earn a scanty respectable subsistence." During the war's course, the petitioners noted, the cost of "board, provisions, and all other articles of female consumption" increased "an average of at least seventy-five per cent." And for reasons unexplained, the petition offhandedly comments more than complains that

*Filling Cartridges at the United States Arsenal at Watertown (Mass.).* Woodcut illustration by Winslow Homer. *Courtesy of Eon Images.*

women had actually suffered a 30 percent reduction in pay. Maybe feeling embarrassed at having to state the obvious to the president and fearing that their credibility might be in doubt, the petitioners humbly noted that "it is perhaps superfluous to say, that it has produced great suffering, privation, and, in many instances, actual hunger. Such, however, is the truth." Their request was for "IMMEDIATE AID," and their wish was that "it be done without delay." Figuratively throwing themselves at the mercy of the executive, the women concluded with an eloquent nineteenth-century flourish:

> *Trusting in the generosity of your nature, the justice of our cause, and the claims which our sacrifices have given us, we confidently leave the issue in your hands, praying that the God of the husbandless and fatherless may so incline your heart, that your answer may shed light where all is dark; send joy for sorrow; and sunshine and peace to the thousands that are now bowed by cloud and storm.*

Characterizing the petition as "certainly true in equity," Lincoln forwarded the document to Secretary of War Stanton, asking that "the case be fully examined" and "so much relief given as can be consistently with the law and the public service."

# A MOST DANGEROUS JOB

Easily lost in the discussion of wage discrimination and long workdays is the issue of danger.

In November 1862, some forty men, women and girls were killed when a Confederate arsenal in Jackson, Mississippi, exploded. In a cartridge assembly room, granules of gunpowder stuck to the bottom of a pan of wax used to waterproof cartridges. When the container was placed over a burning candle to melt the wax, the clinging particles ignited, setting off a fiery chain reaction of death and destruction.

In March, just four months later, a second Confederate arsenal exploded, this one in Richmond, Virginia. In attempting to remove a stuck friction primer, a device used to fire a cannon, Mary Ryan, an eighteen-year-old Irish immigrant, tapped the primer a few times on her worktable. This coaxing, as gentle as it was unwise, flashed the primer's powder. The resulting spark spread not only fire and smoke but also unimaginable agony and widespread death. By the time the coals had cooled and the death knell rung, Mary and

Ruins of the Richmond Arsenal, Richmond, Virginia. *Courtesy of the Library of Congress.*

forty-four of her co-workers were dead. As in Jackson, the victims were girls, young women, a few boys and some men. And whether curse or coincidence, this fire raged on an unholy Friday the Thirteenth.

Catastrophe was not the sole domain of the South, however. Farther north, in Pittsburgh, where the Ohio collects its life force from the generous contributions of the Allegheny and Monongahela Rivers, an arsenal disaster lay in wait for its own careless youth or distracted laborer. The wait ended on September 19, 1862. Springless wagons loaded with barrels of gunpowder rode hard over the cobblestone streets of the fortress-like Allegheny Arsenal. The jostling and bouncing of poorly assembled barrels leaked granules of black gunpowder into the streets' stony crevices. Explosive material lying loose in the streets of a working arsenal was a safety hazard well known to nineteenth-century laboratory superintendents. A popular remedy was an arrangement assigning staff to sweep clean the routes of traffic. In Pittsburgh, this work was halfheartedly done by adolescent and teenage boys. On an autumn day, when neglect randomly trumped diligence, the iron shoe of a draft horse grazed the top of a loaf-shaped cobblestone, flashing a spark that ignited a small but critical accumulation of spilled gunpowder just as the floorboards of a powder delivery wagon passed over. By the time the explosions ceased and the flames were snuffed, seventy-eight people were dead. Of these dead, seventy-two were women and girls. And still there were other incidents. In Philadelphia, the Bartholow Cartridge Manufacturing Company exploded on March 29, 1862, killing and wounding over sixty people. In Waterbury, Connecticut, another civilian cartridge-making plant exploded on April 1, 1864, killing four and destroying the facility.

These were tragedies not unknown to the Washington Arsenal workers and their families. Even the two Southern events would have been noted in greater or lesser detail in local news accounts and street-side gossip. In a war that famously pitted brother against brother, direct family ties between the arsenal workers in Richmond and Washington, only some seventy-five miles apart, would have been neither impossible nor improbable.

A link with the Allegheny disaster is more certain and direct, however. In the aftermath of the Pittsburgh explosion, the Washington workers took up a collection from among their poorly paid ranks and sent a contribution of $170 to help with the relief for the victims' families. A response, expressing the Pittsburgh workers' gratitude for the concern and generosity of fellow workers so far removed from the effects of the tragedy, arrived in the Washington Arsenal's mailroom on the morning of June 17, 1864. Many would never live to hear the expression of appreciation.

## CHOKING TO LIFE

By 11:50 a.m., with breakfast long past, the Choking Room women savored the relief promised by the approaching midday dinner break. The muggy June weather was oppressive, as cool off-river breezes were few. With the laboratory's few high windows and three doors propped open, the building looked as if it were a trap set for any cooling remnants the month of May might have left behind. If the cramped room had no fan and the overhead sun no mercy, the women's fashions showed little compromise to summer's, or work's, discomforts. The dark hues of their cotton summer-weight dresses seemed too Northern for a city so far south. Underframes of metal hoops supported additional folds of stifling material from waist to gaiter-topped shoes. Sleeves, long and puffy, filled-out high-necked blouses whose buttons were tiny and plentiful. Long stockings and ample undergarments added a second body-covering layer demanded by nineteenth-century assumptions about modesty and hygiene.

An unidentified woman dressed in contemporary clothing for women during the Civil War, taken between 1860 and 1863. *Courtesy of the Library of Congress.*

Industrial design contributed little to the women's comfort. That a roof and four walls protected them from rain and snow seemed only coincidental to the army's need to keep the linen-wrapped cartridges and their powdered components dry. A product mostly indifferent to ambient heat and cold meant that the effects of those elements on the workers were of secondary concern. No overhead fans circulated the trapped heat of summer, just as no space-heating stoves slacked the chill of winter. Random outdoor breezes and whiffs of heat seeping from standing stoves in adjacent gunpowder-free rooms were welcomed but unintended benefits.

The women labored through their twelve-hour shifts sitting shoulder to shoulder on long wooden benches with no back supports. The use of a communal bench, rather than individual chairs, meant that once the women were positioned, it was practically impossible for those in the middle sections to leave their seats without disrupting the work of all the other women. To have enough room to stand, a woman would have to push the bench backward to clear it from beneath the protruding lip of the worktable. Such a maneuver, however, could be executed only in coordination with all her seatmates. Once standing, decorum demanded that she file out toward one end or the other of the bench, a move that had to be done in conjunction with her co-workers moving out of her way or, awkwardly, by sliding between them and the table edge. Modesty, fashion and space constraints eliminated the manly option of simply swinging a leg over the bench and stepping out.

Inconvenient as were the cramped and discomforting working conditions, the constant irritation of an aching back, a full bladder or an overheated room might have helped mitigate an otherwise immobilizing fear that the nature of the work would naturally arouse. In a time when the street sightings of the empty sleeves and stiff-legged gaits of wounded, blue-coated veterans confirmed newspaper reports of the devastating effects of modern ordnance like that which they assembled, the annoyance of minor discomforts must have been a welcomed distraction.

In the course of a day, all the women found themselves surrounded by danger in the form of spilled traces of gunpowder and packed cases of cartridges. Off to the side, but always close at hand, were boxes of powder-filled cylinders, open at the top and needing only a bullet and a choking twist of thread to ready them for their death-dealing mission. In ironic phraseology, the Arsenal women worked daylong and year-through to choke inanimate cartridges to life. A thousand chokes over several hours filled a crate with the cigar-shaped .54-caliber ammunition. Each round was laid neatly inside a box set within the reach of a bloused arm. One round lay next to the other until the bottom tier was complete. The bottom rank formed a foundation that supported a second layer and so on until the box was filled with one thousand. Whether first in the box, or last, each round lay by design, snug and secure, with the bullet head pointed back at the worker.

With the clock approaching noon and the thermometer passing ninety, the subject of food and where to eat lunch in the draining June heat might have dominated the thoughts, if not the conversations, of the laboratory women. In Superintendent Brown's laboratory, thoughts might be free, but conversations were not. Safety, Brown knew, demanded that the women's minds be focused on the dangerous work at hand. The record was clear that, if chance and carelessness were the vanguards of death and mayhem, undiverted attention was the remedy. Silence, or at least the absence of ongoing chatter and casual conversation, was demanded. Enforcement, however, was selective. While talking was discouraged, singing was permitted and, if done well, probably encouraged.

But this day, Friday, June 17, once the work had stopped and cool lunch spots had been claimed, conversations were sure to bemoan Brown's stern dismissal that morning of one of the laboratory's young workers. An Island family would be denied a gregarious girl's steady, albeit modest, income for the seemingly insignificant act of talking and laughing too much. In a peculiar quirk of fate, an old man would fire a young girl, and both their lives would change irrevocably.

## SPONTANEOUS COMBUSTION

While doing little for the spirits of his workforce, the broiling June heat facilitated the drying of Superintendent Brown's fireworks. They sat undisturbed—and unobserved—in the sun-drenched out-of-the-way spot Brown favored for the task, between the laboratory's south wall and a small magazine some thirty feet away. The pans' copper frames, efficient conductors of heat, were painted black to augment their heat-absorbing characteristics. All morning, as the sun's rays intensified, the blackened pans' heat-soaking attributes worked as efficiently as the best of Superintendent Brown's cartridge chokers.

At some point that morning, earlier than Brown anticipated, the flare material ceased being damp and began to bake. Perhaps if Mr. Brown had not selected his isolated spot so well, a passing teamster, a young messenger or an official on his rounds might have asked him about the slender whips of smoke wafting from spilled powder granules along the edges of the pans.

Perhaps if Brown had been a scientifically educated chemist rather than a self-taught pyrotechnist, he might better have appreciated the need for careful observation rather than casual inspection.

Perhaps if Superintendent Brown had been less prone to spectacular but unannounced firework tests, someone might have told him that he should check those three pans of stars smoldering down behind the Choking Room.

But the spot was isolated, and Brown was self-taught, and whether planned or not, Brown's periodic, unannounced spectacular displays of red and white star flares were well known. So now, nobody knows for sure when the first star pellet reached its tinder point and flashed from harmless smoldering to life-stealing spark. Eighteen-year-old Clinton Thomas may have been the first to notice. Thomas, working in the gun-carriage shop to the south of the laboratory, was looking directly toward the back wall of the cartridge room when he saw something explode, sending fiery streamers arching skyward and red and white trails of phosphorus rocketing as far as James Creek, some forty feet to the east. For a second, Thomas thought Mr. Brown was setting off fireworks. In another second, he knew he was wrong—frightfully wrong.

Staring at the same wall, but from the other side, inside the Choking Room, sixteen-year-old Henry Seufferle didn't recall hearing an explosion. Engaged with his work sweeping the floor, he was looking out the back window from a position across the room, close to the door. Suddenly, swiftly and to him, silently, a firebrand blazed through the high window and flew into the room. Seufferle ran for his life, trailing a loud howl intended as a warning.

At the same instant, Superintendent Brown and his assistant, Andrew Cox, were chatting with Major Edward N. Stebbins.[5] Both the old man and his young assistant stood, while Stebbins, the Arsenal's military storekeeper, sat in a chair behind his worktable near the front of the Choking Room.

The glint of something out of the ordinary streaming past the rear window caught Stebbins's eye. Sliding back his chair, Stebbins excused himself and left the conversation to step outside for a better view.

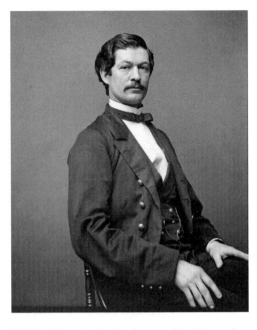

E.N. Stebbins (undated). *Courtesy of the Library of Congress.*

Above the drone of Brown's casual business banter, Cox heard Seufferle's alarming holler. Glancing across the Choking Room and through the open back window, he saw a streak of a bright and glowing flash, followed, as with an uncomfortably close lightning strike, by the powerful wrath of a thundering explosion. He turned to run. It was 11:50 a.m., and for twenty-one young women, death was closer than the afternoon dinner break.

## THE FIERY SERPENT

Maggie Yonson, Bridget Dunn and the dozen other women on the south side of the long Choking Room table couldn't see what Henry Seufferle and Andrew Cox saw. With their backs to the window and their attention on their work, they were oblivious to the spectacular shoot-up flashing just beyond the wall a few feet behind them. Across the table, the women's view through the head-high window was better only when the demands of their finger-nimble tasks relented enough for an upward glance. However, if Melissa Adams, Annie Bache or any of the others on that side of the bench had had a chance to look toward the window, they would have seen the tiny fuses of burning star material shoot through the open casement and silently land on their tabletop. The ensuing chain reaction, blazing bright and furious among the tiny sprinkles of gunpowder that littered the surface of their workspace, would have been the last thing the two girls ever saw. The sun-bright flash coursed like a "fiery serpent" down the table, blinding many and, as they responsively raised their arms to shield their eyes and protect their faces, set alight the puffy sleeves of their cotton dresses. Having reached the table's edge, neither satiated nor extinguished, it moved laterally, following the powder-crumb trail to the first of the twenty-nine cartridge-laden boxes that sat inches to the front of each woman. At that time of day, the boxes would have been half full with five hundred lead-tipped, linen-wrapped cartridges snuggly housing fifty grains of highly combustible gunpowder. The resulting explosion lifted the roof from the building and set the room aflame.

## From Laboratory to Crematory

In the time it took for a heart to skip a beat, the Choking Room went from an uncomfortably hot workspace to a metal-melting inferno. To the non-discerning human ear, what sounded like a single blast was, in fact, a series of near simultaneous explosions of growing intensity.

Superintendent Brown's fiery serpent sparked along the cluttered table-top, devouring spilled granules of gunpowder and following the most defined powder trails, like some bullet-stealing snake finding its way into the nest of freshly hatched choked cartridges.

Effervescent sparks would, at random, sting the thin linen skins of the cartridge casing and, burning their way through to the core of highly flammable powder, explode. Unencased by a carbine's muzzle, however, these weakly confined explosions, sounding more like a firecracker's pop than a rifle's bang, shot their lead bullets sluggishly against whatever was closest while, more dangerously, shredding the wrappers and igniting the powdery contents of the other nested cartridges.

These little explosions, the first of the series, quickly raised the cartridge box temperature past its ignition point. Now, rather than isolated discharges, fourteen thousand cartridges in some two dozen half-filled ammunition boxes erupted simultaneously with a blast powerful enough to blow down the building's brick and frame walls. This was avoided when the blast vented upward, lifting the 2,400-square-foot tin roof off its footings and dropping it back again. The blast, transforming what once had been an efficient, if uncomfortable, work site into an improvised crematorium, generated a scorching fireball that shrouded the workbench and rocketed the room's ambient temperature to over three thousand degrees. As the temperature dropped as quickly as it rose, every mundane item in the room suddenly seemed intended to meet the needs of the voracious flames. Straw hats and summer bonnets, oaken benches and poplar boxes, sheets of correspondence and shelves of inventory books, ink wells and glue jars, all provided fuel to the spreading fire. All this, and little more than a second had passed.

## THE SOUTH SIDE OF THE TABLE

How Julia McEwen, Emma Tippett and the ten other women on the south side of the table died is not clear. Trapped in the narrow space between their workstation and the back wall, they may have scarified any precious seconds of grace granted them between life and death, struggling to slide their benches back the few inches that would give them space enough to stand and run. In this futile struggle, all prayerful families begged that in the end, their loved daughter, sister, wife or sweetheart did not simply burn to death in the intense heat. Most mercifully, and highly probable, death likely came quickly when, with their last breaths, the startled women inhaled a lungful of super-heated oxygen and instantly seared useless that life-sustaining organ.

Only three of those who worked that side of the table survived: Ada Webster, Sarah Gunnell and Minnie Mitchell. The record is unclear as to why fate placed them out of death's reach that day. It is known that seventeen-year-old Ada Webster was at home when the explosion occurred. Why she was not at her work station is unrecorded, but if she was the girl of gay spirits Brown sent home for talking and laughing too much, her light heartedness may well have saved her life.

Perhaps because twenty-three-year-old Minnie (Wilhemina) Mitchell and nineteen-year-old Sarah Gunnell were sitting near the open end of the bench, they were able to free themselves from the dead zone burning over the table and make their way out of the building. While badly burned about the face and arms, Minnie was taken to her home, where family care helped her to survive.

Having made it through the flames and out the Choking Room door, perhaps a step or two ahead of Minnie Mitchell, Sara was helped from the laboratory's porch by two men. "Terribly frightened" and "badly burned,"

Sara fled the Arsenal grounds and ran to her home several blocks up 4½ Street. Once in the safety of her family, she fainted, giving rise to initial reports that she had died.

Whether for reasons of agility or reflexes, nineteen-year-old Emma Baird, one of eight children and the last woman seated on the south side of the table, the one to whom location should have given a life-saving advantage, never made it out of the building and would, in death, be unidentifiable.

## THE NORTH SIDE OF THE TABLE

Across the table, the devastation, while less deadly, was no less widespread. The first three women—Kate Brosnahan, Lizzie Lloyd and Melissa Adams—never made it out of the building.

Kate Palmer, the next in line, won her race with death by jumping out the laboratory's rear window and, in the process, impaling her neck on a piece of iron. Thrice blessed, she survived the explosion, the fire and her neck wound.

Rebecca Hull, sitting next to Kate, despite being severely burned about the face, managed to make it out the door along with seventeen-year-old Annie Bache, twelve-year-old Sallie McElfresh and Catherine Goldsmith, whose age is unknown. Outside, Rebecca was taken home and would die there the next morning. Due to the extent of their burns, Annie, Sallie and Catherine were taken to the nearby Arsenal Hospital. And while Ms. Goldsmith would survive with scars forever embossed on her face, arms and hands, neither Annie nor Sallie would live through the night.

Pinkey Scott, the widow with two young children, was, at thirty-one, among the oldest women in the room. Although she would escape the explosion and make her way outside, she should have died inside the room alongside Kate, Lizzie, Melissa and the others. Having been knocked unconscious by the blast, Mrs. Scott found herself on the laboratory floor, entangled among and beneath the bodies of a half dozen of her workmates. Freeing herself from the weight of the pile, she fought her way out of the burning building and immediately fled, running north up through the Arsenal yard. Only as she approached the front gate did she become aware of a searing pain and discover that her legs were badly burned and blistered. Taken to her home, she survived, but only for three torturous weeks. In early July, pain and infection took their toll, and she died, orphaning a thirteen-year-old son and his five-year-old sister.

## DEATH BY MEDICAL TREATMENT

An unfortunate situation with the art of medical care during the Civil War was that the attention given a seriously burned victim in a hospital, whether military or civilian, differed little from what a family could provide in the familiar comforts of home. In either place, a victim's survival prospects were not particularly good.

Advice in the Union's Ordnance Manual of 1862 recommended that burns be covered with fresh lard and bandaged with linen soaked in a formulated mixture of "sweet oil" and "hartshorn," "well-beaten together."

An item in an 1864 edition of the *Evening Star* reported that "Dr. Hall" believed the "best and most accessible (burn) remedy in the world" was to "thrust the injured part in cold water…and cover the part an inch or so deep with common flour." Full benefits would result if the victim would "live mainly on tea and toast, or gruels, and keep the bowels acting freely every day, by eating raw apples, stewed fruits and the like." Dr. Hall concluded with the enthusiastic endorsement that "no better and more certain cure for scalds and burns has ever been proposed."

For more serious situations, the burn victim's pain was neutralized with doses of laudanum, an inexpensive opium and alcohol solution readily available, without prescription, at any neighborhood pharmacy. The burns themselves were bandaged with soft raw cotton or cotton lint that was regularly dampened with cool water to keep the wound "clean and sweet."

Although a well-intentioned and widely used intervention, it was a procedure, like most others of the time, that did more harm than good. Ignorance of germ theory by both medical staff and concerned family, compounded by fly infestations, low levels of personal hygiene and the deplorable sanitary conditions in Washington, meant that damp bandages trapped water contaminated by animal and human waste atop the fire-damaged skin. Leaching infectious bacteria through the wound, any patient surviving the burn trauma was likely to die from infection.

## THE NORTH SIDE OF THE TABLE, PART II

Also trying to escape the confines of the north side of the table, but unable to make it through the life-granting door just a few unobtainable yards away, were thirteen-year-old Emily Collins and Mary Burroughs. More fortunate were their tablemates, Dona Clements, Florence Kennedy, Jane Shilds and

Sara Kidwell, each of whom survived. A telling example of the battle they fought with the searing fire and intense heat that beat down one frightened young challenger after another was the evidence brought out by twenty-three-year-old Sara. Displaying the severe burns typical of Arsenal survivors, there was no doubt that Sara's hands, face and arms took the brunt of the blast. Afterward, however, as her family cut away the charred shreds of her cotton blouse and the folds of her expansive hoop skirt in preparation to treat her wounds, they found that Sara had endured heat so intense it had melted blotches of lead onto the fabric of her clothes that then simmered their way through to the surface of her skin.

Of the twenty-nine women in the Choking Room at the time of the initial explosion, only twelve were able to traverse the twenty-some feet from their seats at their worktable to the sanctuary of the fire-free space just outside the walls of the laboratory. Not to be discounted in tallying the Arsenal's death toll is the role fashion played in hindering the safe exit of the women from the room. The expansive dress of the day—the puffy, long-sleeved blouse and, more particularly, the space-robbing spread of the hoop skirt—was an ensemble suitable for only a measure-treaded stroll on an open promenade. Rapid movement anywhere, let alone through a workroom cluttered with fiery debris, was awkward at best and promoted foot-tripping stumbles and knee-dropping falls. In addition to restricting movement, once set in motion, the bulky dresses careened wildly around the legs and, unless consciously restrained, bumped haphazardly against furniture and furnishings bordering the scope of its sway. In a social setting, this was merely inconvenient and easily controlled. In a fire-filled room, it was dangerous and deadly. With every item in the laboratory aflame, be it worktable or sunbonnet, cartridge box or lunch basket, bookshelf or pocketbook, open flames narrowed escape routes to slender fire-fringed paths through, over and around burning obstacles.

And as the women ran the fiery gauntlet, their bulky summer skirts—thin, paper light and barrel wide—erratically brushed against the flaming fabric of a sister's dress or the hulk of a burning cartridge box and burst into flames. Spreading as if it were some fiery strain of virulent infection, the slightest contact communicated disfiguring burns and pain-racked deaths from one skirt to another.

With the promise of cool, fire-free air beyond the door or out the window, the women ran and clambered as best they could in a race with the flames burning through the thin layers of cloth that modestly sheathed their frightened selves. And waiting outside for the heartbreaking few who broke through the fiery barrier were their shocked and confused male colleagues.

The last person to enter the Choking Room had been Major Stebbins. Puzzled by flashes of light crossing the edges of his peripheral vision, Stebbins had interrupted his desk-side conversation with Superintendent Brown and his young assistant, Andrew Cox, to walk outside and investigate. Stepping off the shaded porch-like loading dock into the bright near-noon sun, he sought a broader perspective of whatever was happening behind the building.

The record is unclear as to whether he returned from his brief exploration satisfied, confused or distressed by the untimely fireworks display. Return he did, however, perhaps wondering how he would explain to the roomful of women just why he was closing the building's rear windows at a time when the noonday sun would make an uncomfortably hot workroom unbearable. As he stepped onto the porch, the laboratory in front of him exploded, blowing shut the Cartridge Room door and spreading fire throughout the building. Rushing forward, he burst open the door whose threshold he had

Some of the male Arsenal workers. *The Washington Arsenal Manufactory Women Killed in the Explosion, (circa 1864). Courtesy of the National Archives and Records Administration, College Park, Maryland. Still Photo Division.*

so recently sauntered, feeding the inferno a fresh stream of oxygen and causing two more boxes of cartridges to explode.

This counter-instinctive action of running into a fire rather than away from it, may have helped save the lives of the Choking Room's few survivors. By bursting open the front door—one of the few escape exits available to the trapped women—Stebbins may have gifted them precious seconds in their desperate dash for non-scorching air. With the door open, the survivors were not slowed by having to stop and fumble with it.

One saved by Stebbins's action may have been Superintendent Brown. With strangely worded comments in the aftermath, Brown was able to note a distinction between hearing the explosion and experiencing its bone-jarring effect. In perhaps one of the Arsenal incident's greatest understatements, Brown reported that he "noticed" the explosion and started to "come out" of the building, but that in "a measure" the jar of the explosion forced him out. Safely out of the flame-engulfed and smoke shrouded factory, with Cox securely in his wake, Brown saw men he knew only as blacksmiths, carpenters, wheelwrights, teamsters, office assistants and invalided soldiers converging on the laboratory, seemingly pulled by an unseen force in the inferno's core. As with Stebbins, they ran toward the fire rather than away. No observer would mistake these men for mere gawkers; their pace was too purposeful, their carriage too urgent and their faces too anguished. For these tradesmen, laborers, clerks and soldiers were the brothers, fathers, friends and neighbors of the young women who needed their help, as never before, if they were to survive.

## WHAT THEY SAW

The explosion, oddly muted for such a powerful blast, sounded an alarm that all Arsenal workers dreaded and to which all responded. Putting aside whatever work was at hand, the men ran toward the source of the sound and the cause of the alarm. Once outside the confines of their workshops, there was no doubt as to what needed to be done. Although only seconds had passed since the dull thud echoed off the walls of the Arsenal's brick and frame buildings, orange flames reddened the edges of the jet black tower of smoke that radiated out of the laboratory's high-set windows, totally obscuring both its pitched roof and a wide swath of the mid-morning's blue sky. Even as the dense smoke spewed out the top half of the window frames, a stream of seventy frightened women fought their way out of the doors and

Stone carving depicting smoke billowing from the burning laboratory, from the monument to the women killed in the Washington Arsenal explosion, at Congressional Cemetery. *Photo by Brian Bergin.*

over the sills of every window on the north end of the laboratory, injuring backs and breaking bones in the process.

This drama unfolded in stark contrast to the dazed and desperate few staggering from the Choking Room at the southern end of the building. But whether north or south, east side or west, via door or window, an all-too-common scene was the plight of women running from the disaster with their wide-silhouetted skirts and their ruffled blouses ablaze. In reaction to the horror before them, workmen grabbed the nearest flame-cloaked woman and did what they could to smother the fires that fed on the light cotton fabric. With bare hands, some ripped away burning cloth; others threw canvass tarpaulins over those too distressed to drop and roll. One lifted a young woman off the ground and carried her some fifty feet to James Creek, where, like a revivalist preacher, he submerged her into its saving waters. Cox, blown out of the Choking Room along with Superintendent Brown, emerged to find two startled women standing on the porch washing their hands. Reacting more quickly than they, he was able to push both women off the steps and out of harm's reach.

Unique of the rescuers, perhaps, was Hosea Moulton, the Arsenal's chief clerk.

As with Brown and Cox, Moulton too was in the Choking Room at the time of the explosion, although standing apart from the two men at some

Judge Hosea B. Moulton in his later years. Pictured with John L. Clem on November 11, 1925. *Courtesy of the Library of Congress.*

point closer to the women working at the cartridge assembly table. After the explosion, in the midst of the rush for the door, Moulton stopped long enough to lift up one of the burned girls and carry her out of the building, despite damage done to his hands, chest and arms. Years after, he would report that victims had only seconds to make good their escape before the entire room was in flames. And as if to emphasize the inherent danger in the era's fashions, he noted explicitly that the clothing of the girl he rescued was afire, while making no similar comment about his own clothes. For reasons unspecified, Moulton never identified the woman he saved that day.

From his position in front of the laboratory, Stebbins was able to assist in the rescue of over thirty women, including some whose burning clothes were extinguished only after they were wrapped in a tarp. As with Moulton, many other men that day would suffer painful upper body burns.

Valiant as were so many of the men, they were not responsible for all the rescues. Quite simply, many of the women, through heroic effort and pain-stifling determination, saved themselves. At one point, thirteen women who made it out of the flames left the terrifying scene in a group. Frightened, but not panicked, they ran to a tugboat docked alongside the Arsenal wharf rather than to the more distant front gate. With all safely aboard, they sailed up the Potomac to the Fifth Street wharf, where they were met and taken home by friends and family.

# THE FIERY HULK

In minutes, all who could were out of the inferno, while those who couldn't remained where they fell and died. The injured and maimed were sheltered under the shade of dusty roadside elms. The distressed were comforted, at least initially, with the gentle touch of rough hands and the soothing sound of baritone voices. The Arsenal Hospital's staff, including surgeon James Porter and a young civilian doctor from the Island neighborhood, Charles Allen, provided what medical assistance they could.

Dozens of Arsenal laborers and close-by Island residents flooded around the site inquiring after the fate of relatives and neighbors. Because so many survivors had fled and flames kept rescuers away from the interior of the laboratory for over an hour, it initially proved impossible to compile an accurate list of the living and dead. Instead, rumor, guesses and speculation fed both the gossip mills and the newspapers. Three boys feared dead turned out to be merely missing for a brief time. Miss (Emma) Carr, said to be among the fatalities, was thoroughly frightened and shocked but thankfully alive and well. Millie Webster, frequently referred to in news accounts as Ada, died several times in the newspapers, despite the fact that she had not even been at work that day.

While survivors were being comforted and reporters misinformed, the laboratory continued spewing its mournfully dark shroud of smoke unchecked into the afternoon sky. Fortunately, ringing the Arsenal compound were several private fire companies, all of which responded with alacrity and apparatus enough to restore order to the chaos that reigned over the center portion of the Arsenal. Directing streams of water onto the laboratory's fiery hulk, in an unusually coordinated way, were the hand-pumped fire wagons from the normally aggressively competitive station houses of Columbia, Perseverance, Anacostia and Franklin, along with a unit from the American Hook and Ladder Company. The urgency of the circumstances, augmented by the intimidating presence of Secretary of War Stanton, army chief of staff Henry Halleck, Ordnance Bureau chief General George Ramsay and

Arsenal commandant Major James Benton, may have accounted for the fact that the crews focused on fighting the fire rather than each other. In operation too, were the government's big steam engines, the Rucker, the Meigs and the Hibernia, whose powerful hoses cooled down the nearby magazine, powder room and vulnerable wood-frame shops and outbuildings. This unusual display of cooperation successfully eliminated the threat to the hundreds of people milling about the still dangerous site of a second and larger explosion. In fact, there was a second, although thankfully muted, explosion that harmed no one and merely spewed burnt timbers and smoldering debris a few feet into the air.

Through a combination of luck and hard work, the conflagration that started just before noon was contained and extinguished by 1:15 p.m. With the fire quenched, Major Benton ordered that the coroner be summoned and the grim task begun of sifting through the laboratory's crumpled walls and charred hulk for bodies.

Ruins of the Washington Arsenal Laboratory after the June 17, 1864 explosion. *Courtesy of the National Defense University, Library Directorate, Fort McNair, Washington, D.C.*

# THE GRIM TASK

One of the first actions taken in the wake of the explosion, after the Arsenal's direct telegraphic link with the War Department had alerted Secretary of War Stanton to the disaster and the additional medical help requested, had been to secure all access to the Arsenal grounds. Uncertain at the time as to the cause of the explosion, Confederate sabotage was not an unrealistic presumption. Regardless of the reason for the blast, the emergency would not be helped if the Arsenal grounds were inundated with distraught parents and concerned neighbors seeking after the well-being of one of their own. A contingent of the distinctively clad, sky blue–jacketed Veterans' Reserve Corps (VRC)—soldiers recuperating from war wounds and temporarily assigned to this light duty unit until again deemed combat ready—was ordered to close the Arsenal gates to all but essential personnel. The effect was to build a common ground of concern just outside the Arsenal walls as anguished mothers and fathers, sisters and brothers, relatives and friends waited for word about a loved one on the inside.

Too soon, disturbing information poured from the gates. First came Pinkey Scott, in her burned and smoke-stained dress, fleeing the smoldering destruction in the vain hope of outrunning the pain spreading up her blistered legs and across her worried face. Then came others in singed coveys of frightened girls, clinging together for strength as they instinctively stumbled away from the fire and toward the safety of home and the comforting embrace of a relieved family. The many scenes of joyous reunions and sorrowful revelations outside the northern gate were heart rendering in the extreme.

At the ruins, the company of invalided VRC soldiers gently moved survivors and laborers alike to spots away from the crumbled walls of the laboratory. A wide cordon would give searchers the space they needed to lay out and identify the bodies of victims now buried in ash and debris. It would not be long before they realized that disturbingly little space would be needed.

An observer of the search would, at first, be puzzled by the procedure. In some cases, searchers would stop and stoop down to more carefully examine the ashes at their feet. After a hushed discussion between partners, one would move carefully out of the ruins and return with a stretcher-like, straw-covered board. Together they would slide on to it what passed for a body and carry it to the open area where it would be placed on the ground and covered beneath a large tarp.

More puzzling, however, were the increasing number of occurrences in which the partner returned to a discovery carrying not a long board but, more simply, a large box and sometimes a small pan. These, too, were reverently brought out and placed under the canvass.

In total, seventeen bodies were found and laid out for identification. Several were picked from the ruins still encircled with the mangled wire frames of hoop skirts, an anguishing contrast to fashions so recently thought attractive. Many remains were merely torsos, disjointed from the other parts of their bodies. Placed under the tarp, too, was an eighteenth box that held nothing but miscellaneous body parts and bone fragments associated with no particular body.

Regardless of the size of the burden, each time remains were carried to the tarp, the crowd surged forward with hopes of recognizing a missing loved one. Standing firm against this grieving onslaught, the wounded soldiers of the VRC were well enough to hold the periphery of the open-air morgue against this mournful assault.

Even before the tarp was lifted for the sake of identification, it was clear that, in too many cases, it would be accessories and remnants, rather than facial features and hairstyles, that would aid recognition. No amount of mental preparation, however, could prepare parents for the horror awaiting them when the soldiers pulled back the canvas.

Ann Arnold, the forty-five-year-old widowed mother of Emma Tippett, fainted as she unsuccessfully searched the makeshift morgue for a recognizable sign of her daughter. She was carried to a nearby building to recuperate and adjust to the fact that neither she nor anyone else would ever again see a face they recognized as that of their beloved twenty-three-year-old Emma.

Johanna Connor, however, was identifiable, but only by a belt fragment and a swatch of dress fabric seared to what remained of her body. She was missing the crown of her skull, exposing the charred mass of what was, just a few hours before, the source of lively conversation and youthful dreams.

Someone—an acquaintance perhaps, but one not familiar enough with Johanna to know that her branch of the Connor family spelled the name with an "o" rather than an "e" and had discontinued using the Irish "O'" prefix—penned a handwritten sign, placing it near what remained of her head, saying, as if to the incredulous, "This is Johanna O'Conner." Bettie (Elizabeth) Branagan, Julia McEwen, thirteen-year-old Lizzie Brahler and Emily Collins, Eliza Lacy, Maggie Yonson and Kate Horan were, as with Johanna, identified not by their individual features but by a familiar pattern of cloth, a unique piece of jewelry or, in one case, a pair of gaiter shoes that, because something—or someone—fell over them, escaped being incinerated.

Perhaps most startling of all the identifications was that of Bridget Dunn, by Superintendent Brown. Brown thought a set of intact remains was that of Miss Dunn, he said, because both were "of large size."

Recovering from shock, and her earlier fainting spell at the open-air morgue, Ann Arnold returned home to care for her infant grandchild. Awaiting her, along with the needy child, was the news that Emma's husband, William, had died from wounds received earlier in fighting on the Virginia Peninsula.

## AFTERNOON AND EVENING: THE CASEY INVESTIGATION

While the laboratory still blazed, Secretary of War Stanton wrote a letter to the army chief of staff, Major General Henry W. Halleck, asking that Halleck direct "one or more competent officers to proceed immediately to [the Arsenal to] make inquiry into the cause of [the] explosion and take such evidence thereon as they deem proper and report to this Department." Responding with alacrity hard to imagine for their time, and one not characteristic of his days as a field commander, Halleck had E.D. Townsend of the Adjutant General's Office issue Special Order #210 that very afternoon.

Special Order #210 directed that a three-person board, consisting of battle-tested Major General Silas Casey, Colonel William Maynadier of the Ordnance Department and Colonel Richard D. Cutts, renowned soldier, surveyor and scientist, "immediately proceed to the Washington Arsenal to investigate the cause of an explosion which occurred to-day at that place." The order further directed that they "take such evidence thereon as they deem proper, and…report the result of their investigation to this office."

Arriving at the Arsenal that afternoon, the three officers (the "Casey Board") toured the explosion area and then assembled in an Arsenal office to take testimony.

Setting to work, the board called four witnesses: Major Benton, commandant; E.N. Stebbins, military storekeeper and paymaster; and Thomas Brown and his assistant, Andrew Cox. Of the four, three had been in the laboratory at the time it exploded: Stebbins, Brown and Cox. Only Major Benton had not been on the scene when the building went up in flames.

Although the report indicates that testimony was "concurrent," it neglects to clarify whether this meant the testimony of all four witnesses was taken at one time or whether the four testified consecutively at the same Arsenal location. Regardless of how the testimony was taken, the report, in summarizing its investigation, chose not to preserve any direct quotes, individual remarks or personal comments.

With no equivocations such as "about" or "approximately," the board stated that "there were twenty-five (25) girls and women employed" in the Choking Room, with another 79 in other parts of the building, a combined figure of 104 endangered workers.

The panel reported that in the process of sun drying "a very large number of rocket stars" at a spot "directly opposite to the southern windows of the choking room," the stars, composed of nitrate of strantia, chlorate of potash and gum copal, "ignited by spontaneous combustion." Hedging its conclusion somewhat, the panel added, "Or from other cause [sic]." It did not speculate as to what that other cause might be.

Regardless of the cause, the panel reported that "a part of one" of the stars was "drawn into the nearest open window of the choking room, [and] lodged among the cartridges, a box of which was placed in front of each operator, and set them on fire. Almost instantaneously the fire was communicated to the other boxes and hence, the explosion. The fire spread rapidly and soon the entire building was in flames."

The panel added that fire suppression and rescue operations started immediately, and "every effort was made to rescue the inmates and extinguish the fire."

In summarizing its conclusions, the Casey board said it "has no doubt from their careful examination as well as from the testimony they took, that the explosion in the laboratory was caused by the ignition, from spontaneous combustion or other unknown cause, of the rocket stars drying near it."

Despite having "no doubt" as to the cause of the explosion, the board softened the definitiveness of its conclusion by saying, "An accident from such a cause is not known to have heretofore occurred." There was, however, some comfort to be taken from the fact that it also believed a similar accident "probably would scarcely ever occur again."

The panel concluded its report with the seemingly self-evident recommendation that orders be given to the effect that "dangerously combustible material" not be dried in the vicinity of any site where munitions are produced. They did not, however, assign blame to any specific individual or recommend that any further investigations be undertaken. In the same vein, their report contained no fatality count, casualty list, estimate of damage or comment on the Arsenal's ability to function in the aftermath of the explosion. Nonetheless satisfied with an afternoon's work, the panel sent its three-page, handwritten report to Colonel Townsend before sunset on the smoldering ruins of the laboratory.

## The Coroner Takes Charge

It was 4:00 p.m., and steam-like wisps of dark smoke still skulked skyward from the wet and crumbled ruins. Under the merciless afternoon sun and the soot-smudged sheet of white canvas, the seventeen lay morbidly still, as if patiently waiting for someone to take them home. Should it have been so, the wait was over, for the coroner had arrived. The District's coroner, seventy-one-year-old Thomas Woodward, did not live on the Island. He maintained a large household, consisting of his wife, Octavia; his thirty-three-year-old son, Thomas; Thomas's wife and their two young children; and his nineteen-year-old youngest son, Roswell, in the affluent crosstown neighborhood of Georgetown.

Having been summoned by Major Benton, Woodward immediately impaneled a twelve-member jury of inquest from the ranks of the District's blacksmiths, stonecutters, painters and clerks and set to work.[6] As with the Casey panel, the jury's first task was to view the remains. In the interval since the retrieval efforts' end, the numbers of spectators milling about the guard line who had not seen the specter under the canvas had grown significantly. Woodward ordered the tarp pulled back, and the shock of seeing the effects of death by fire could be measured by the spontaneous requiem of startled gasps, spirit-broken moans and body-shaking sobs. It was a chorus of realization that these charred torsos, exploded skulls and piles of disassociated bones were all that remained of the dutiful daughters and the hardworking women who just a few hours before were so ordinarily alive. With the blackened pile of spilled bricks and splintered timbers in the background, Woodward retreated to an isolated spot with a bevy of jury members and witnesses in tow and began taking testimony.

First to testify was the pyrotechnist, Superintendent Thomas B. Brown. He explained the work process and clarified that the women were engaged in the sole task of making cartridges. Somewhat defensively, perhaps, he noted that, although there may have been one or two rockets in a desk drawer—certainly no more than three—the women were not involved with

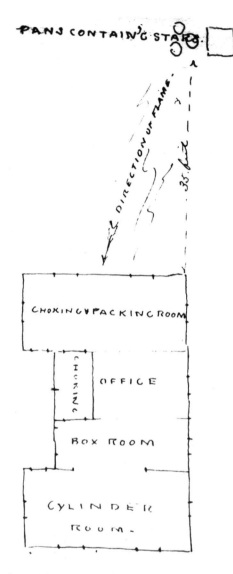

General Ramsay's sketch of the grounds showing pans near the laboratory. *Courtesy of the National Archives and Records Administration.*

the manufacture of any type of firework, other than cartridges. Mixing two different types of manufacturing would have been against orders.

He told the jury that he had placed the rocket stars in copper pans to dry between eight and nine o'clock that morning at a spot about thirty-five feet behind the laboratory near the white picket fence that ran north to south behind the laboratory.

Not only had he placed the material there that morning, but this was also his favorite spot for drying stars; he had used it often—even in August, Washington's hottest and most uncomfortable summer month—and had never had an accident. He also pointedly testified that he had never been told not to use the site. Furthermore, there was little danger in putting the material there, he felt, because it was of a type that would not explode if accidentally impacted. As if to support his cautionary nature, he told the coroner that he even used a powder mixture of his own design rather than that called for in the commandant's manual because he believed his formula to be safer.

Finishing his testimony, Brown noted that although he was in the laboratory at the time of the explosion, he did not know whether the stars or the cartridges had been the cause. Called next was the Arsenal's commandant.

Major James G. Benton, commandant of the Arsenal, had not been at the laboratory at the time of the explosion and, as he explained, arrived at a point when all those inside were certainly dead. Whether it was too late for the women, Benton's first concern was preventing the spread of the fire to a nearby magazine and other flammable Arsenal buildings. Despite the raging fire and a minor, secondary explosion of what were probably those few rockets that Brown had stored in his desk against regulations, Benton successfully managed to see the conflagration safely extinguished. Exploring the site afterward, the major testified that he found the flare pans overturned on the ground and coated with a white residue. The white deposit indicated to him that the pans had been the source of the explosion. It was his opinion that the black paint on the pans absorbed the sun's heat and, through a process of spontaneous combustion, ignited the stars. And although this was his conclusion, he did not know whether it was an opinion Mr. Brown shared.

Continuing, Benton noted that he frequently inspected the laboratory and regularly emphasized to Brown the importance of safety. His injunctions, however, were cautionary and not the result of any violations for which Brown was responsible. The major described Brown as a "good practical chemist" and a "careful and competent man," even while characterizing him as "imprudent" for the quantity of stars he placed together in the three pans. The fact that the pans were placed where they were, Benton felt, was not intentional on Superintendent Brown's part but an oversight. He added that Mr. Brown was not a "scientific man."

Interrupting, even though he was not a sworn witness and was not giving testimony, General George Ramsay, the head of the Ordnance Department and Benton's immediate predecessor as commandant of the Arsenal

Major James G. Benton, commandant of the Arsenal. *Courtesy of the Archives, Springfield Armory NHS, U.S. NPS.*

General George
Ramsay. *Courtesy of
National Archives and
Records Administration.*

reminded Benton—and in so doing, informed the jury—that, in fact, it was customary for Brown to dry his flare material at this site.

Major Benton also testified about the effects of choked cartridges on the women sitting just a few feet away from the open, half-filled ammunition boxes. Noting that the heads of the bullets were pointed directly at the workers, he believed that "at the time of the explosion more or less injury was done to the girls by their being struck by these balls as the cartridges exploded." Although there was no evidence offered to support this position from witnesses, survivors or forensic reports, Benton's statement reflected the limited understanding of fire characteristics prevalent at the time. Indeed, it would be another century before fire management engineers would convincingly demonstrate that fire victims faced far greater dangers from heat, suffocation and poisonous gases than from the effects of loose ammunition.

Young Henry Seufferle, perhaps one of the three boys hired to help out around the laboratory and the sole son of a widowed German immigrant, testified that he had seen the three copper pans behind the building. He estimated that each contained two to three hundred stars. He also recounted that he ran outside after seeing the blaze come through a window at the south end of the room. In making his successful escape, Seufferle told the jury that he had paused just long enough to help two young women off the laboratory's porch and to see two other men help carry away the injured Sarah Gunnell. He was unable, however, to identify the remains of any of the victims. Henry was just sixteen years old.

As with Seufferle, Andrew Cox, Brown's assistant, gave his perspective of the explosion and testified that he thought the three copper pans contained a total of eight to nine hundred stars. He then attempted to give an accounting of the women in the Choking Room. However, he was unable to provide an authoritative listing because the fire had destroyed his record books. He did not explain why he could not identify his staff without the aid of a personnel list. Apparently having not given any thought to the need for an accurate roll until this moment, he speculated there were "about thirty girls in the room." However, when iterating a list based on where the women sat, he could recall only twenty-five of their names, including Millie Webster, who was not at work that day. The coroner did not press him for greater detail.

Major Edward N. Stebbins (aka Howard M.), the Arsenal's paymaster and its military storekeeper, testified that he was sitting in the Choking Room talking with Superintendent Brown and Cox. During the course of the conversation, his attention was "pulled" to something flying about outside the window across the room on the south side of the building. Leaving the two men, Stebbins walked out the front door of the room to get a better look at the strange activity. Once outside, he saw "stars flying about." Some, he testified, shot off as far the river, some forty feet away, and were coming from the spot where Brown customarily dried his star material and where for the past two or three weeks these stars had been curing.

As he returned to tell Superintendent Brown about what he had seen, the building exploded and burst into flames. The blast must have blown the doors shut because Stebbins reported that he had to "burst the doors open" in order to get back into the Choking Room.[7]

He went on to report that once the doors were open, and as he was attempting to enter the room, two boxes of cartridges exploded. Perhaps to suggest that fate rather than carelessness ruled the tragedy, he testified that there was no "loose powder" in the room—"unless a cartridge had been accidentally broken." Since he did not continue the thought to charge that there were broken cartridges about, the inference is that acceptable levels of neatness and safety were in effect. Conceding some subtle distinction between spills of "loose powder" and the scattered granules of powder that had, in the course of production, built up on the top of the women's work table, Stebbins noted that once this inconspicuous accumulation of tabletop powder alighted, the fire spread rapidly down the work bench, blinding the workers and setting their clothes on fire. In their frightful quest for help, many of the women ran to the windows seeking to escape and, in their haste, spread the fire from their burning garments to the dresses of others. Perhaps because it was obvious to all present, he did not elaborate on his statement that he felt all the women on the south side of the bench had died where they sat. Although unable to get back into the cartridge room, Stebbins testified that he had helped about forty women escape from the building and, using a tarpaulin, was able to help extinguish the flames of those whose dresses were on fire. Having nothing further to add, he was dismissed.

Clinton Thomas, an Arsenal laborer and the last witness, viewed the explosion from outside the laboratory and some distance away from the building. From his perspective, he could see sparking behind the laboratory's south wall and, unconcerned, thought that Mr. Brown was setting off some fireworks. No sooner had the thought passed than the building burst into flames.

# THE JURY RETIRES

At this point, Coroner Woodward told the jury that the testimony of the several remaining witnesses would serve to corroborate the testimony they had already heard. Responding to what may have been interpreted by the jury as a subtle cue from the coroner that additional testimony would add nothing to what they had already heard, the jury reported that it felt further testimony about the explosion unnecessary. It did, however, want to hear from some of those who had identified the victims. Three witnesses testified how bits of fabric and jewelry had helped them identify Johanna Connor and Margaret (Kate) Horan. In addition, there was the previous testimony from Superintendent Brown as to how he had identified the remains of Bridget Dunn. With no new information available about the explosion, its cause or the effects, the jury retired to the commandant's office for deliberations.

# THE VERDICT

How long, and in what depth, the jury discussed the questions of the accident is not recorded. There is no evidence, however, to suggest that the process prevented any of the jurors from being home in time for their evening supper. If the jury had need for clarification, substantiation or reiteration, neither the press nor the public record reflected that uncertainty. After what was ambiguously described as only "mature deliberation," the jury returned with a verdict explaining what caused each of the then-known seventeen deaths and who was responsible for them. The verdicts differed only in that two of the readings replaced the generic phrase "the body of a female" with the names of Johanna Connor and Margaret (Kate) Horan. The verdict read:

> *That the body of a female came to her death by the explosion of the laboratory of the Washington Arsenal, where she was employed choking cartridges; that the said explosion took place about ten minutes to 12 n., and it was caused by the superintendent, Thomas B. Brown, placing three metallic pans some thirty feet from the laboratory, containing chemical preparations intended for the manufacture of white and red stars; that the sun's rays operating on the metallic pans caused spontaneous combustion, scattering the fire in every direction, a portion flying into the choking room of the laboratory through the open windows, igniting the cartridges and causing the death of the said deceased. The jury are of the opinion that the superintendent, Thomas B. Brown, was guilty of the most culpable carelessness and negligence in placing highly combustible substances so near a building filled with human beings, indicating a most reckless disregard for life, which should be severely rebuked by the Government. They also find that the deceased had no property.*

# GOING HOME

With the approval of the coroner, the families of Johanna Connor, Catherine Horan and Bridget Dunn were allowed to carry home their straw-lined boxes of charred remains, as if the macabre proof might somehow soothe the doubts of incredulous kin. Improvised funeral processions moved resolutely, by foot or wagon, from the laboratory's circle of death out through the anxious crowds at the Arsenal's north gate. Passing somberly up $4^{1}/_{2}$ Street, able-bodied siblings, comfort-giving neighbors and helpful bystanders respectfully marched the makeshift coffins off the Island and to the doors of humble homes on Massachusetts Avenue, English Hill and Capitol Hill. For these few, grieving would be a private family matter. But not for all.

## UNIDENTIFIED BUT NOT UNLOVED

Left behind on the Arsenal ground were the remains of Melissa Adams, Emma Baird, Kate Brosnahan, Mary Burroughs, Susie Harris, Lizzie Lloyd, Ellen Roche and Emma Tippett, all of whom were burned beyond recognition. No features, no clothing remnant, no distinctive shape identified these women to the loved ones who had known them all their lives and could be expected to grasp any trace of the familiar that would help bring closure to these tragically interrupted lives. But try as they might, these families would go home without even a tin pan of remains to help staunch their grief.

For the family of Melissa Adams, the burden of her death was laden with tragic coincidence. Within the past two years, Melissa was the third of the Adamses' seven children to die violently. A few months after a brother had accidentally shot himself hunting, another was killed when he was run over by a coach. For the superstitious of Washington, Melissa's death was especially haunting since all three accidents occurred on Fridays.

For reasons unstated, but eminently understandable, the families of Lizzie Brahler, Bettie Branagan, Emily Collins, Eliza Lacy, Julia McEwen and Maggie Yonson chose to leave the identified remains of their daughters behind and to take home only their unanswerable questions and their spirit-breaking grief.

## TWO TELEGRAMS TO THE ARSENAL

Distraught as they were, a degree of comfort was provided the distressed families by Secretary of War Stanton's telegraphed directive to Major Benton, informing him that the War Department would assume all funeral expenses for the Arsenal women. Furthermore, Benton was told, he should "not spare any means to express the respect and sympathy of the Government for the deceased and their surviving friends." That sympathy and respect was, in part, demonstrated immediately when all labor at the Arsenal was suspended for the next workday, a Saturday.

A second telegram also awaited Benton's attention. News had arrived from the Watervleit Arsenal in New York State reporting that a fire had broken out in its blacksmith shop earlier in the morning. The situation turned precarious when work crews refused to fight the fire out of fear that the magazines might explode. The fact that there was no explosion, that no one was killed and that the property damage was relatively minor was due to the timely arrival of three steam engines from the nearby city of Troy. For a day saddened by so much tragedy, the telegrams were granules of good news.

Evening arrived at the Arsenal grounds soon after the Jury of Inquest left. By then it was clear that no more improvised coffins would be carried home to crepe-draped lodgings. Instead, when the shroud of white canvas was lifted for the last time, the remains of each victim were carefully wrapped in blankets, placed in wooden boxes and carried inside the carpentry shop in one of the nearby frame buildings. There, these fourteen dead would spend the first night of eternity together among damaged gun carriages and the heavy tools of the arms trade. A night guard of the walking wounded protected the charred remains from both the insensitivities of the ghoulish and the inconsideration of the curious. Now, whether by directive or default, the government assumed the responsibility, as well as the expense, of ensuring that the eight unidentified dead and six identified boxed remains were respectfully buried. Showing an unusual sensitivity for the memory of the dead and the needs of their families, the government then stepped respectfully aside and allowed a self-selected cadre of Arsenal workers to manage the details of their co-workers' funeral. The workers began immediately and spread the word, through broadside postings, social networks and workplace grapevines, that there would be an early morning meeting at the Arsenal for all those laborers not needed at a family wake, viewing or visitation.

And so the murderous sun set on the wreckage of Washington's greatest Civil War disaster, leaving in its cooling ebb and lengthening shadows mournful islands of incredulity, grief and the comfort of age-old funerary rituals.

# 3
# Saturday, June 18, 1864

## Organized Labor: The Workers Take Charge

Oblivious to the unfolding paradox that, in hindsight, highlighted the gender biases so prevalent during the era, men—brave, kindhearted and well meaning—assumed the lead in coordinating the public display of grief. Women, dominant in managing the funeral rites of hearth and home, would dutifully accept supportive roles in the planning and execution of the spectacular mass demonstration.

Tamping down their personal grief, the burned and bandaged workmen of the Arsenal met early Saturday morning. There was much to do, and time was precious. Poor as it was, the Island neighborhood was blessed with an abundance of organizational talent. There were charismatic community leaders, men in charge of work gangs, labor leaders from the skilled craft trades and ward politicos. In an era when distressed families needed emergency help and individuals sought the protection of friends, organizational membership was common. The banners and flags of the Sons of Hibernia, the Temperance Society, the Republican Party, funeral societies and oddly named fraternal lodges were widely recognized and ardently respected for the good they did their members in times of need. But over and above the social and service aspects, these clubs taught their members how to organize themselves to accomplish a common goal. These were men who knew how to conduct an orderly meeting and appreciated the value of a clear motion, properly seconded, and a well-led committee. No one needed to tell them how their energies might best be used to aid a community in distress or a member in need. Now, called by grief, guided by respect and questing for a lasting touch of dignity, these latent talents would be brought to the fore.

First to arrive at the Arsenal's carpenter shop on Saturday morning was the forty-nine-year-old Irish immigrant Peter McGuinnis, overseeing a skilled crew of joiners and painters. Today, however, instead of assembling caissons and building limbers, they assumed the solemn responsibility of making the coffins for the dead they once knew as co-workers and neighbors. The coffins were to be made of poplar and hand stained. Inside, each would be lined with muslin, white satin and gimp. On the outside, there were silver-plated handles and a "coffin plate" with the victim's name, when known. For those who could not be identified, the simple word "unknown" would be as close as the dead women would come to having names.

As the guildsmen set about their tasks, their colleagues were assembling in a nearby workshop. Once seated, focused and open for business, Joseph A. Burch (aka Birch), a thirty-two-year-old Arsenal tinsmith, moved that Mr. Henry Dudley be made chair and chief marshal of the funeral. The motion passed unanimously, with William Toppin elected to serve as secretary.

John (Henry) Dudley, a gun-carriage builder, must have been an extraordinary man. Not only did all of his colleagues think highly enough of him to choose him to lead this very complicated tribute, but he had also distinguished himself by accepting severe burns as the price for saving at least one of the fire-shrouded women the day before. Dudley was a fifty-seven-year-old Island resident who, with his fifty-four-year-old wife, Drucilla, had four children ranging from twenty-five to seven. Two of the children were girls of the same age as some of the younger victims whose funeral he now oversaw. On assuming the chair, and the responsibility for ensuring that the varied assignments were completed in a neat and timely fashion, Dudley stated that the object of the meeting was to "take some actions concerning the recent explosion." More specifically, he suggested that committees be formed from the various Arsenal workshops to arrange for: 1) the collection of relief funds and 2) burial of the victims.

One of the first orders of business was a status report on the explosion's victims. By Saturday morning, the count stood at eight dead, whose bodies would never be identified; six identifiable dead at the Arsenal; two hospitalized girls—Sallie McElfresh, twelve, and Annie Bache, seventeen— both of whom died during the night; one, twenty-year old Kate Horan, who was taken to her in-laws' home and died surrounded by family; three (Bridget Dunn, Johanna Connor and Rebecca Hull) whose remains had been taken home after the coroner's inquest; and more than a dozen other women who had survived the fire but were injured to a greater or lesser extent. This included Mrs. Pinkey Scott, Catharine Goldsmith and Catharine Cogan, who, although severely burned, still lived.

Committee representatives from each of the Arsenal's main workgroups— clerks, saddlery, machinists, blacksmiths, carpenters, tinners, painters, armorers and laborers—were identified as ready for assignments.

Next, a motion that every man connected to the Arsenal contribute one day's pay "to defray expenses" was passed unanimously. Whether this motion was literally intended to apply only to the male workers at the Arsenal is not clear. However, given that the customs of the day found the exclusion of women from this committee acceptable, it would not be unreasonable to assume that the words were intended to be taken literally.

A committee of three, consisting of the representatives Burch (tinners), Isdell (laborers) and Reilly (armorers), was authorized to select an appropriate grave site in the Congressional Cemetery.

Representatives King (blacksmiths), Stahl (machinists) and Colison (carpenters) were to procure hearses, appoint pallbearers and direct the funeral, which, it was decided, would start at Arsenal grounds at 3:00 p.m. the next day, Sunday.

Messieurs Hickman (saddler) and Barry (painters) were to visit the families of the dead to let them know of the committee's plans and to arrange for their attendance at the funeral.

Dudley also offered the thought that there would be strong support within all the departments—indeed, with the citizenry in general—for a "fundraising effort to have a monument to the women who lost their lives in the employment of the government" erected over the grave site. A committee for this task would meet once the funeral was done and everyone was back at work on Monday.

There was also unanimous agreement to a resolution memorializing the fact that, as a sign of respect for the dead and injured, all Arsenal labor was suspended for the day.

The meeting adjourned with everyone appreciating that a lot of work needed to be accomplished within a very narrow opportunity window of twenty-plus hours.

## THE FUNERAL ROUTE

The simplicity of the assignments belied the complexity of the mission. Committees were broken down into subcommittees and subcommittees into workgroups. In a city rife with ceremony, parades and pageantry, the

Arsenal's clerks and tinsmiths stepped out with focus and determination to initiate the incremental steps that would culminate in one of the largest funerals the nation's capital had seen to date.

Building around the known centers of activity—a funeral service on the grounds of the Arsenal and burial in Congressional Cemetery—the funeral committee marked out a procession route. From the Arsenal's main gate, the procession would move north through the Island neighborhood along 4½ Street, past the edge of the Mall a few blocks east of the Smithsonian, over the stagnate waters of the Washington Canal and to the point where 4½ Street intersected Pennsylvania Avenue—a distance of slightly more than a mile. At Pennsylvania, the procession would have to make a sharp, oblique turn to the right, changing its orientation from due north to southeast. For the next several blocks, the cortege would be marching directly toward and then, as it moved through a slight bow in the road, alongside the Capitol. Past Capitol Hill, the procession would continue straight on Pennsylvania Avenue for a mile to the circle where it intersected Georgia Avenue. Angling to the left, the mourners would march north and east along Georgia for three blocks to the cemetery gates on E Street.

The route was not the shortest distance between the two points. Rather, this was a procession intended to be seen and appreciated by as many people as possible. It would move through the Island neighborhood of friends and relatives, to the expensive hotels and residences near the Capitol and through the economically and racially mixed communities beyond.

By immediately establishing the course of the funeral march, the local papers would have time to publish it in their afternoon editions, while still allowing fraternal groups time to pass the information on to their members.

## SPECIAL NEEDS

In the workshop, carpenters were updated on the number of coffins needed and the Arsenal location where a platform would have to be constructed for the next day's service. Not only would the stage have to be built from scratch, but it would also have to be respectfully decorated, necessitating that appropriate quantities of flowers and bunting be purchased and arranged.

Since one hundred yards separated the building where the remains of the victims lay and the spot where the funeral service would be conducted, a crew of teamsters and their wagons would be needed just to move the coffins within the Arsenal grounds.

For transportation beyond the Arsenal's walls, the committee needed to obtain, in addition to a fleet of hearses, more than two dozen wagons, carriages and buggies to transport the victims' families to and from the cemetery.

Reflecting the religious makeup of the victims, a Catholic priest and at least one Protestant minister were needed, as was a program, an overall timetable and the order of march. Invitations had to be extended to Arsenal officials and government dignitaries and the protective ranks of the Veterans' Reserve Corps requested. The District police needed to be informed of the procession route and its cooperation obtained to maintain order and control traffic.

The role of fraternal groups needed to be determined. Six pallbearers were required for each coffin and their role rehearsed prior to the start of the funeral. And still, the list continued.

Even as the planning and preparations progressed, circumstances changed. The families of Rebecca Hull, Kate Horan and Johanna Connor chose to have home services on Saturday, followed by private burials in the Catholic cemetery of Mount Olivet. This suggests that at least some of the Catholic families preferred to have their daughters buried with a religious service in consecrated ground rather than in a secular cemetery. Although the three services were separate, it was arranged for the hearses of Kate and Johanna to meet at the intersection of Massachusetts and New Jersey Avenues and, in their own two-hearse cortege, proceed easterly to the cemetery.

The family of Bridget Dunn chose to have a private funeral on Sunday afternoon at the same time as the public ceremony at the Arsenal. Leaving from her home on Capitol Hill, Bridget's hearse would proceed south a half block or so to Pennsylvania Avenue and respectfully wait while the bodies of the last people she saw on earth passed by. Turning to a tack somewhat to the north and east of the main funeral route, the friends and family of Bridget Dunn, riding in some twenty carriages, would retrace the mournful path to Mount Olivet traversed just the day before by the grief-laden friends and families of Bridget's Catholic co-workers.

Services for twelve-year-old Sallie McElfresh would be conducted by the Reverend Mr. Lemon of the Island's Ryland Methodist Chapel on Sunday. Sallie's body, carried in a private hearse and escorted by four pallbearers—including her seventeen-year-old next-door neighbor, Bill Greenwell—would join the main funeral procession at the juncture of F Street and Pennsylvania Avenue. At the cemetery, her coffin was to be separated from the others for burial in a family plot.

The family of Annie Bache, while participating in the public funeral, requested that her coffin be placed in the last hearse so that they could easily claim it at the cemetery and have it placed in a temporary vault.

With its long and complicated list, Henry Dudley, his committeemen and the Arsenal workers would be busy right until the last minute.

In a morbidly ironic juxtaposition of newspaper items, the Saturday edition of the *Evening Star* ran its updated story of the Arsenal explosion next to a quarter-page Fourth of July advertisement emblazoned with the bold, uppercased headline: "FIREWORKS! FIREWORKS!

At 1:00 p.m. on Friday afternoon, reported the *Daily Morning Chronicle*, the thermometer in front of Franklin & Co. Opticians on Pennsylvania Avenue registered 110 degrees. For those familiar with the city's wilting weather, it was unnecessary to add that it was also very muggy. For Dudley, and the planners of the next day's procession, it was hoped that Sunday would be no worse.

# 4
# SUNDAY, JUNE 19, 1864

## THE FUNERAL

By noon on Sunday, it was, again, oppressively hot. Comfort could be taken, however, in the fact there had been no additional deaths overnight and that all the assignments for the mass funeral had been successfully completed. Nonetheless, despite the grand plans, the early arrival of hundreds of mourners at the Arsenal's closed gates was unanticipated. Soon after morning church services and breakfast rituals, individuals and families began congregating outside the Arsenal's shuttered north gate, as if unaware of, or oblivious to, the widely circulated announcement that the procession would begin at 3:00 p.m. But by 2:00 p.m., over one thousand people were pressing against the gate expecting admission. And even though the press of the crowd and the heat of the afternoon sun drove many of the darkly clothed mourners away from the gate to shadier spots along the Island's dusty streets, a throng remained waiting, more or less patiently. At 2:30 p.m., the gates were opened, and like a torrent of murky water, the mourners flowed in, battering some against the gate's now-too-narrow portals.

Wisely in hindsight, but for reasons both practical and convenient, it had been decided that the service would be held at an open site directly behind one of the storehouses in the northern sector of the Arsenal rather than at a more distant southern location closer to the scene of the accident. This served the double purpose of keeping the crowd away from the military portion of the post, while reducing the distance the mourners would have to walk in the afternoon heat.

The Washington Arsenal's North Yard, where the funeral took place. *Courtesy of the Library of Congress.*

Once through the gate and on the Arsenal grounds, the visitors saw a cordon of light blue–coated VRC troops protecting a raised platform, roughly fifteen by twenty feet, covered with black-edged duck cloth and canopied by a mourning-draped American flag. Resting on the stage were two rows of identical handmade silver-trimmed coffins. Each was bedecked with wreaths and bouquets of colorful summer flowers, white lilies and red roses, made by the Arsenal's female employees. Arrayed on the north side of the platform were the coffins of Melissa Adams, Emma Baird, Kate Brosnahan, Mary Burroughs, Susie Harris, Lizzie Lloyd, Ellen Roche and Emma Tippett. Sisters in death, all eight of the polished coffin plates were etched with the same heartbreaking surname "unknown." To the south, the sun glinted off the little-girl names of daughters somehow recognizable to family: Annie Bache, Lizzie Brahler, Elizabeth (Bettie) Branagan, Emily Collins, Eliza Lacy, Julia McEwen and Maggie Yonson.

As more people filled the viewing area, the job of the VRC became harder. Co-workers and neighbors unintentionally jostled the guards and pressed their ranks as they sought to touch the coffins that held the remains of dear friends and next-door neighbors. The wounded soldiers struggled to keep the spectators back from the stage, while holding open a space around the platform reserved for families of the victims. As the grieving families were respectfully ushered in, they began moving from coffin to coffin looking for the loved ones they had lost. Discoveries were signaled by peals of anguish rising about the mingling din. Heart-stuttering sobs and despondent moans were associated with those families whose darlings lay in one of the coffins marked "unknown." The family of Annie Bache pulled at her coffin and begged that they be given one last chance to look at her. Delicately, they were diverted away with their pleas unanswered. Eight-year-old Anna Adams managed to clamber onto the platform in a fruitless search for her unidentified sister, Melissa. Frustrated and overwhelmed, she fainted and had to be carried out of the congested area to recover. Passing the ranks of coffins, family members would gently touch the wooden lids, accepting an imperfect comfort from this last fleeting gesture of physical contact.

Between the coffin rows sat the invited dignitaries: General George Ramsay, chief of the Ordnance Department and former commandant of the Arsenal; Major Benton, current Arsenal commandant; Major Stebbins, military storekeeper, witness to the explosion, rescuer and near victim; Surgeon Porter, an angel of mercy to the wounded and dying; and Ordnance Department officers Lieutenants Prince, McKee and Stockton. It was not reported whether Thomas Brown was in attendance.

## LINCOLN'S CONSOLING GESTURE

A prominent spot, near the front of the platform at the edge of the crowd, was held in ready for the guest designated "Chief Mourner." A military entourage bordered the enclave sheltering the three men moving to its center. The tallest silhouette was unmistakable and the second vaguely familiar, while the third was not identifiable. Whether invited or of his own volition, President Lincoln was present with his secretary of war, Edwin Stanton, and Stanton's son, Edwin Jr. The significance of the president's visit was not lost on most people present. Since the typhoid death of his eleven-year-old son, Willie, in February 1862, President Lincoln had attended but two funerals: one for his friend, the poet and soldier General Fredrick W. Lander, and the other for Stanton's infant son, James, who died from a smallpox vaccination. Both funerals had been in 1862.

This, then, was Lincoln's first public funeral since his son's death. Clearly this was a significant event to Lincoln and to those who saw him there. Modern cynics might construe the visit as little more than a calculated attempt by a desperate president to gather votes for the approaching November election.

Such a conclusion, however, would need to ignore the fact that a constitutional amendment giving District residents the right to vote in a presidential election would not be approved by Congress for almost another one hundred years. Also of note is the fact that, if Lincoln were playing to a nationwide audience, he would certainly have given a speech and been seated in a more conspicuous spot. Yet he was not honored on the platform nor listed in the program. Fairness demands, then, that his visit be seen for what it was: an expression of grief by a parent who knew firsthand the suffering in the hearts

Edwin McMasters Stanton, seated, with his son Edwin Lamson Stanton. Photo taken between 1852 and 1855. *Courtesy of the Library of Congress.*

of those who had lost children in this tragedy. This is borne out by the company he chose to keep for the afternoon. Of all those Lincoln could have traveled with, it was Stanton, a father still affected by his son's death some two years prior, who came with him. Under such circumstances, it is hard to see Lincoln's visit as anything less than a sincere gesture of affection. Surely, Lincoln understood that in coming to this funeral, the families of the victims would know that, in a nation numbed by slaughter, there was still compassion enough in its weary leader for the tragedy of innocents.

Lincoln's presence confirmed the solemnity of this tragedy to be of a magnitude worthy for all, regardless of station, to interrupt their personal routines for brief reflection and public obeisance. The human toll of the Civil War was nearly unbearable, and now fate demanded another usurious installment that neither prayer nor hope could mitigate. The best of the limited options available to a suffering people from the war-torn country's depleted supply of national virtues was the poorly appreciated gift of Perseverance. For surely, only time and grace could assuage the despair that had so recently scorched the hope and hearts of a people already burdened by the vicissitudes of a hard life. And in human form, no man better personified its qualities than did the haggard countenance of the tried and tested president mourning with them that hot afternoon. Whatever their silent disappointment with a seemingly indifferent God, both the bereaved families and a bewildered city asked little more than a sign from the stoop-shouldered president that, pressed with the weight of all his other burdens, he—and through him, the nation—still had strength enough to help carry the weight of their Job-like trials.

## "A Blissful Immortality…"

Once the distraught families were positioned and a relative order established, Father Bokel, the newly installed pastor of the Island's Catholic parish, St. Dominick's, began the service. In a ritual comforting to the many Catholic families present but perhaps disconcerting to the reformation sensibilities of the Baptists, Methodists and Presbyterians in the crowd, Father Bokel recited the Catholic burial service in Latin and respectfully, although indiscriminately, sprinkled the coffins with holy water. Commenting on the flower-bedecked manifestations of death surrounding him, Father Bokel attempted to redirect the attention of the assembled mourners from their personal grief for their daughters and friends to a narrower awareness of the individual's readiness to meet an unexpected death. Concluding with a reminder to the diverse congregants of Matthew's cautionary lesson that death's arrival was often untimely and unannounced, he turned the improvised pulpit over to his Methodist-Episcopal colleague, the Reverend Samuel. V. Leach of the Gorsuch Chapel. The Reverend Mr. Leach began:

> Then I saw a great white throne and him who was seated on it…And I saw the dead, great and small, standing before the throne, and books were opened…The dead were judged according to what they had done as recorded in the books…and death and Hades gave up the dead that were in them.

Moving from scripture to a theme of comfort and consolation, Leech asked the parents, siblings and friends to put aside gloomy thoughts of this event as a tragedy. Better, he said, to see it as an accident that caused no harm to the spirits of the dead: "It was a mistake to regard as of serious importance the mere incidents connected with death." Granting that it would have been of more comfort to the parents if they would have had the opportunity to be by the sides of their dying children "as they made their adieu," there was, nonetheless a "consolation" for them. Comfort would be found in the realization "that those who believed in Christ were not harmed by death, and scarcely felt the touch of fire before they were hastened to a blissful immortality."

To the broader community of congregates, Reverend Leach reminded them that God regularly used the death of an individual to speak to them. Yet the "commonness" of an individual's passing "makes but a slight impression when coming singly." Reaching his eschatological thesis, Leach said:

> *For our good God causes these terrible visitations to come upon us. Let us be instructed by it, and avail ourselves of the time granted us to make character for eternity. May God bless us, and lead us by his counsel to be ready to depart with joy and not grief!*

Leading a recitation of the Lord's Prayer, he concluded with the fervent invocation: "Oh God, thou hast appeared in our midst. The rumbling of thy car hast been heard. Have mercy on us, may our sins be taken from us. Bless the friends of those who have been taken away. Bless their co-laborers and let all classes profit by this dispensation." Content, perhaps, in a belief that neither the parents nor the families of the dead needed a special blessing, and that further celestial petitions were unwarranted, the Reverend Leach relinquished the podium to the procession's chief marshal, the goodly Henry Dudley.

With bandaged hands, Dudley now put in motion his committees' processional choreography. The fruits of thoughtful planning were immediately apparent. With one simple instruction that "the friends of the deceased should enter the carriages and fall in after the hearses and ambulances," the hundreds began an orderly exit, knowing exactly where they should go.

At the Arsenal's gate stood a column of fifteen funeral carriages: a rank of solemn, glass-sided, undertaker-type hearses, alternating with four-wheeled, canvas-topped army field ambulances. In its search for hearses, the committee had found that there were not enough available in the District. Benefiting from the city's abundance of military hospitals and Secretary of War Stanton's directive concerning the funeral, the army was able to assist with the loan of eight ambulances.

As the assembled moved to their modes of transportation and took up position behind the forlorn hearses, a phalanx of blacksmiths, carpenters, teamsters and clerks moved onto the platform. These workmen from the

Arsenal were augmented by a member cohort from the Sons of Temperance, there in deference to Susie Harris, Bettie Branagan and Eliza Lacy, each a member of its ladies' auxiliary. Breaking into paired clusters of six plus one, the men positioned themselves around the coffins and, in march-step, solemnly began moving them to the hearses. Making straight the way, Sergeant Philip Hepburn of the District's Tenth Police Precinct, with a full-strength squad of patrolmen, opened a path through the sea of the exiting mass. Julia McEwen, Emily Collins and Bettie Branagan were the first to be moved; Annie Bache, in deference to her parents' wish for burial in a temporary vault, was, for the sake of convenience, the last. As the hearses and ambulances filled, the procession began to take shape according to plan.

In the lead position, from one of the most modern military hospitals in the District, was the Finley Hospital band. Directly behind it, dressed in white, were several divisions of the Sons of Temperance. This included Excelsior No. 6, to which several of the victims belonged; Good Samaritan No. 1, with its ladies' auxiliary; Equal No. 3; Armory Square No. 4; Columbian No. 5; Aurora No. 9; and Lincoln No. 11. Following the Sons and their ladies, and leading the column of hearses in a carriage of his own, was Reverend Leach. Immediately behind the hearses, in the carriage of the Chief Mourner, were President Lincoln, Secretary Stanton and Stanton's son.

They were followed by the Arsenal officers: General Ramsay, Major Benton, Major Stebbins, Dr. Porter and the three Ordnance Department lieutenants.

Next were throngs of friends and relatives of the victims traveling in all manner of cart, wagon, carriage and hack. In a show of worker solidarity and public compassion for the dead women, District hack drivers had gotten together and agreed to charge those attending the funeral their lowest rates. With about 150 hacks in the funeral procession, the rest of the city was left stranded and virtually hack free for the rest of the afternoon.

Employees of the various Arsenal workshops had organized their own transit operation, including the use of a number of ambulances, and under the auspices of a designated coordinator from the shops and departments, blacksmiths, saddlers, armorers, painters and laborers arranged for all their fellow workers to get to and from the funeral.

The Adams' Express Company, the largest express service in the eastern Union States and a company frequently in and out of the Arsenal gates, provided a large wagon pulled by six white horses tacked out with mourning gear for a contingent of its employees. There is no known family connection between the owners of the company and the victim Melissa Adams.

Mixed among the wagons, carriages and hacks in great numbers were individuals on horseback and small groups of pedestrians. The gathered mass was so large that, once in motion, over thirty minutes passed from when the Finley Hospital Band stepped out to when the last of the mourners began moving up along 4½ Street.

And even in motion, the cortege was not complete. As it moved north from the Arsenal and passed F Street, the hearse with the remains of twelve-year-old Sallie McElfresh slid into line, bringing along with her and her family the Reverend Mr. Lemon, the minister from Ryland Chapel who had conducted her private funeral service; her undertaker; and a corps of young pallbearers, including Sallie's neighbors: seventeen-year-old William Greenwell and two Hall brothers, twenty-one-year-old George and twenty-four-year-old John.

The emotion along the processional route was extensive and demonstrative. The sidewalks were crowded with graven-faced onlookers, as were the windows and rooftops of the homes, boardinghouses, brothels and hotels bordering the Via Dolorosa. Bells in the steeple of St. Dominick's and the watchtower of the Columbia Fire Company tolled as the hearses passed. When the procession reached the sharply angled turn onto Pennsylvania Avenue, opening the grand eastern vista dominated by the alabaster glow of the Capitol, the children of the Wesley Chapel Sunday School, assembled street-side earlier by its superintendent, B.F. Gettings, began singing a traditional funeral shape note hymn in its unique notation of eights and sevens. Haunting, with its "Amazing Grace"–like melody, the children sang:

*Sister, thou wast mild and lovely*
*Gentle as the summer breeze*
*Pleasant as the air of ev'ning*
*As it floats among the trees.*

*Peaceful be thy silent slumber,*
*Peaceful in the grave so low;*
*Thou no more wilt join our number,*
*Thou no more our song shall know.*

*Yet again we hope to meet thee,*
*When the day of life is fled;*
*Then in heav'n with joy to greet thee,*
*Where no farewell tears are shed.*

Nineteen-year-old Susie Harris, one of the unidentified, had been an active member of the school and, if not for the whim of a mysterious Providence, might well have been in choir with them that very Sunday morning. Not only had the children walked the several blocks from the little church to the parade route, waited patiently for the coffins to approach and lovingly sang their moving song, but they had also prepared a written tribute to their lost classmate. Attributing Susie Harris's death to the work of that "mysterious Providence," they gave testimony to her "beautiful character," typified, they felt, by "her punctuality, faithfulness and gentleness as a Sunday School pupil." They took comfort in knowing that although her death was sudden, salvation was eternal.

Although the record is not clear, it suggests that Susie and her younger brother John were orphans living with an adopted family of relatives. The Sunday school testimonial alludes to this when the children offer their sympathy, not to Susie's parents and family, but rather to her "bereaved brother and other relatives."

Having offered their sympathy, the students let the world know that they had taken heed of the disaster and had learned well from it. Closing, they counseled that "as a school we ought to feel ourselves warned by her unexpected removal, to be in future more diligent in every good work, ever ready for the coming of the Son of Man."

Having finished their song, the children, rather than continue to the burial ground, returned to their Sunday school, sang a doxological praise to God and were dismissed to ponder on their own all that the weekend had unfolded before their young eyes.

The procession continued down Pennsylvania Avenue, curving around the south side of the Capitol. Proceeding briskly, yet reverently, mourners passed under the eastward gaze of the newly installed statue of Freedom, standing high atop the Capitol dome. Although soon to change, this funeral was the first major Pennsylvania Avenue processional over which the twenty-foot armed and vigilant bronze goddess reigned. From her vantage point, she could see the crowds moving ahead of the procession, hoping to find an advantageous vantage point of their own at the Congressional Cemetery a half mile distant. Knowing, but silent, her view showed that even at this time, the cemetery yard was already crowded with people who, with the same thoughts of convenience and shade, had arrived hours earlier.

From such a towering prospect, it was also possible to see the unfolding of an inconvenient flaw in Henry Dudley's grand plan. Timing was such that the procession's vanguard was forced to wait, briefly, when it reached the gated entrance to the burial grounds. It had arrived just as the funeral for thirteen-year-old John Carter Jenks was concluding. Logistics were such that the mourners and young John's classmates from the Navy Yard Baptist School needed to exit the cemetery before the Arsenal cortege could enter.

When the passageways cleared, the processionists marched in formal ranks and ambled together in small clusters of mutual support down the bare path leading to the red brick chapel from which humbler connecting walkways radiated out between the rows of substantial family monuments, chiseled modest headstones and open swaths of lawn still waiting to serve. Midway, their route turned right, to the west, toward the mound of dirt that bordered two large open graves near a waist-high brick wall that delineated the cemetery's western flank.

District police officers Phillip Harbin and his partner Joseph Shelton gently moved people along to convenient locations that surrounded the graveside sites reserved for the mourning families, pallbearers, dignitaries and religious officiates. Abruptly, trouble developed when Henry Greenfield, a young man of about nineteen, stood boldly in the center of the path, effectively blocking access to the grave. Unsure of the boy's motivations, Officer Harbin asked him to move. In response to a defiant oath and the boy's arrogant refusal to move, Harbin arrested him. Greenfield, however, resisted, and when Officer Shelton went to help Harbin, Greenfield's friends joined the fray. Order and decorum were restored only after the officers drew their revolvers and marched their prisoners off to jail. It was not reported whether President Lincoln was present for the altercation.

With the pathway cleared and foot traffic moving again, the pallbearers began carrying in the sixteen coffins. Parting forever now from their sisters, the coffins of Sallie McElfresh and Annie Bache were carried to separate burial sites. Sallie was taken to a family plot and buried next to her father and siblings. Annie's family placed her coffin in a public vault in anticipation of a delayed burial in the family plot, perhaps buying travel time for some faraway relatives to attend a family burial.

As the remaining fourteen coffins arrived at the mass burial site, they were lowered one-by-one into the large open graves. Each of the two pits was six feet long, fifteen feet wide and five and a half feet deep. A six-foot strip of grass separated the two. The six known remains, those of Lizzie Brahler, Betty Branagan, Emily Collins, Eliza Lacey, Julia McEwen and Maggie Yonson, were placed on one side of the boundary strip. On the other side went the remains of the eight unknowns: Melissa Adams, Emily Baird, Kate Brosnahan, Mary Burroughs, Susie Harris, Lizzie Lloyd, Ellen Roche and

Emma Tippett. As the coffins were lowered, family members, breaking into loud wails and sobs, crowded the graves' edges calling out the names of their dead and trying to touch the coffins for the last time.

If Christian custom prevailed, the coffins would have been placed facing east so as to welcome the coming of their Christ on Judgment Day. Initiating the final service, Reverend Leach stood as His earthly substitute on the east side of the graves and read the Methodist burial service. Since this was a non-sectarian burial ground, Leach had no Catholic counterpart to balance the service. Filling a broader, nondenominational role, was W.F. Crutchley, chaplin of the Excelsior Branch of the Sons of Temperance. Replacing Leach at the graveside, Crutchley led a call-and-response litany. The assembled responded to each of the chaplin's divine entreaties with the touching call-back: "Farewell sisters, farewell."

Returning to the fore, Reverend Leach closed the service with a traditional benediction and dismissed the mourners to a familiar world now, for many, much changed.

President Lincoln, after dropping Secretary Stanton and his son at their Franklin Square home, returned to the White House. That evening, he and his personal secretary, John Hay, attended a concert of sacred music sung by Madame Cecilia Kreschmar and Messieurs Habelmann and Hermanns. The event, not far from the White House, was performed at one of the president's favorite venues: Ford's Theatre.

He had not been asked to speak at the funeral, and given the customs of the day, there probably was no expectation that he would. But given his somber mood, as evidenced by his presence at both the funeral and the concert, it would not be unfair to speculate that he may well have contemplated the continued appropriateness of his words from just a few days prior in Philadelphia:

> *War, at best, is terrible, and this of ours, in its magnitude…is one of the most terrible the world has ever known…It has…destroyed life and ruined homes…It has carried mourning among us until the heavens may be said to be hung in black—and yet it continues.*

For the families and friends of the twenty-one Arsenal women, the memories of the sunny blue skies of June 17, 1864, were forever to be hung in black. Clearly, the pain of that event could never be shared by those who were not directly affected. Yet solitary as was the family of broken hearts, tender memories could help fill the voids dug by death. Knowing that time would dull their grief, the mothers and fathers, brothers and sisters, friends and neighbors feared it might also steal the memory. The permanence of a loving memorial would help the first and counter the second. Comfort would come to the living by knowing that yet-unborn generations would learn from their now-dead children that things that once happened should never be allowed to repeat. Fortunately for them and for history, the indefatigable Henry Dudley was, once again, en pointe and ready to do his best to help.

# 5

# Monday, June 20, 1864

## Unbearable Grief

A question surely raised in the minds, if not on the lips, of all the families, most of the friends and many of the city's empathetic strangers was, "How—after such a sudden and devastating loss—does a parent pick-up and carry-on?" The answer, dictated by custom and circumstance, would vary from family to family. But for at least one parent, the answer—simple, direct and understandable—was: you can't. On Monday afternoon, at about 2:00 p.m., less than twenty-four hours after her daughter's funeral, the inconsolable mother of Ellen Roche "died of a broken heart."

In circumstances far different than those of the Roche family, death sent the Brosnahan household spiraling into chaos. Twenty-four-year-old Kate Brosnahan was the mother of two children under the age of two. Her husband, Thomas—perhaps responding to the allure of an enticing market price some wealthy Washington draftee was willing to pay for a substitute—had enlisted in the army and left to fight for the Union in the aftermath of Gettysburg. In an era when there was no official protocol for notifying the next-of-kin of a battlefield death, and with no word from or about him for several months, all assumed that Tom Brosnahan was dead. Whatever her actual state, Kate believed herself to be a widow, and this war-widow status may well have been the reason she had been given a job in the Arsenal's laboratory. With her parents, William and Mary Wise, and an aunt, Margaret O'Brien, living near her, it is curious to note that, with her meager wages, Kate nonetheless hired an African American domestic to watch her children while she was at work. And while it was the nanny who was with the children when the news of Kate's death arrived, the aunt immediately stepped in to assume care of the orphans in their "destitute circumstances." As noble and generous as was this gesture, the glow of good intentions was soon washed away by the harsh realities of poor lives gone amuck. At the very time Ellen Roche's mother lay dying of heartbreak, Kate Brosnahan's aunt, characterized in the press as a "common drunkard," was arrested on charges of "abusing her husband." The newspaper report, noting that she had been fined four dollars and required to post a good behavior bond, observed that she was, of course, "unfit to be the children's guardian." That obligation would be assumed by Kate's parents.

## FUNERAL OBSEQUIES

The District's six Catholic churches scheduled a calendar of requiem masses to be said "for the repose of the souls of the young ladies who…were so suddenly ushered into the presence of their Maker."

On the Island, the pastor of Wesley Chapel, the Reverend Dr. Nadal, informed his congregants that he would "preach a funeral discourse on the decease of Susan Harris, the beloved pupil of [their] Sabbath School."

The *Evening Star* announced that on the "next Sabbath morning," June 26, Reverend Brown, of the Island's Seventh Street Presbyterian Church, would preach "a funeral sermon pertaining to the death of those who lost their lives in this sad catastrophe." Both Emma Tippett and Melissa Adams had been teachers in the church's Sunday school.

## A DEGREE OF INDIFFERENCE

Monday's *Evening Star*, an afternoon newspaper, carried a detailed account of the funeral activities, as well as an informative but oddly flaccid editorial entitled "The Arsenal Disaster." The editor seemed to have had access to a source of information beyond that presented during either the Casey inquest or the coroner's. He noted, without explanation, for example, that this was not the first time Superintendent Brown had had problems with his fireworks material. Describing Brown as an "excellent pyrotechnist, with much enthusiasm for his business," he went on to report that Brown "has come to look upon an occasional blow-up as quite a routine affair."

He also suggested that it was disingenuous for Brown to have claimed that he always placed his fireworks in that very spot to dry. True as that may have been, he had not explained to the jury that it was only in the spring that the old building, originally built to serve as the Arsenal's laboratory, had been reconverted from a storehouse to a cartridge-making facility once again. With that conversion, the once-innocuous building was then in dangerous proximity to any consequences of defective and errant fireworks.

Using language stronger than the coroner's legal description of Brown as guilty of "culpable carelessness," the *Evening Star* characterized him more graphically, as a man possessing a "degree of indifference to human life hard to believe." Disappointingly, the editorial concluded not with a clarion call for a more in-depth federal investigation to identify and eliminate any individual behaviors or organizational factors that may have contributed to the explosion but by wishing Brown "no manner of harm."

Writing as if unaware of, or unconcerned with, the possibility of prosecution under charges such as dereliction of duty, manslaughter or negligent homicide, the paper merely called for an interdepartmental transfer rather than a reform-prompting indictment of those culpably guilty. In the future, the editorial said, Brown should be used in "some department where no such disaster as that of Friday may possibly be again connected with his name." Within the year, Brown was replaced by his assistant, Andrew Cox, as the superintendent of the laboratory. The humiliation of neither the disaster nor the demotion would, however, be enough to drive Brown from his position as the Arsenal's pyrotechnician. The record indicates that he would hold that slot through an 1865 explosion that killed nine men, an 1866 fire that destroyed several buildings in the laboratory complex and on into the next decade. The era of the investigatory journalist had not yet arrived in the nation's capital.

# THE OBSTREPEROUS MR. GREENFIELD

In reporting on the obstreperous Mr. Greenfield and his run-in with the police, the paper noted that Justice Cull had fined him $21.54 "for being disorderly in the graveyard" and held him in jail to ensure his appearance in court on the charge of resisting arrest. Given that the Arsenal women were making less than $1.00 a day, and that the daily pay of skilled workers was between $2.00 to $3.00, the fine was substantial. And though the record of Henry's punishment for fighting with Officer Harbin has been lost to history, we do know that in 1870 he died, at twenty-five, of yellow fever. Perhaps as an indication of his ne'er-do-well lifestyle, he died with no identifiable occupation.

## THE MONUMENT COMMITTEE

Among the weekend accomplishments of Dudley and his committeemen was the distribution of an announcement that the Arsenal workmen were requested to attend a 12:30 p.m. meeting in the gun shop on Monday "for the purpose of devising some means to erect a suitable monument to the memories of the victims of the late disaster." Prompt and methodical as ever, Dudley called the meeting to order and opened the floor to business. A member of the clerks' committee (F. Whyte) immediately introduced a resolution authorizing that a Monument Committee be formed for the purpose of soliciting contributions "from our citizens" to be used to erect a monument in memory of the Arsenal victims in Congressional Cemetery. The resolution passed, and a twelve-member committee was created, consisting of representatives from the various departments, Dudley and Major Stebbins as treasurer.

As its first item of business, the committee approved a circular it wanted published in a number of national newspapers to solicit proposals. It also established a workgroup to oversee efforts to seek contributions, or what it referred to as "subscriptions," from individuals, associations, community groups and businesses. The effect in doing this was twofold; it would, of course, raise the money needed for the monument and, at the same time, undermine the efforts of the District's criminal element to exploit the tragedy by bilking the citizenry of donations collected under false pretenses. An announcement of the start of the fundraising effort was sent to the local newspapers in time for the next day's editions. Included in the notice was a warning to contributors that a number of unscrupulous, irresponsible and unauthorized parties were already afoot in the District. Even as the notices were going out, the committee counted its first success. At Giesboro Point, the great cavalry remount station and horse depot directly across the Eastern Branch from the Arsenal, clerks were already collecting subscription forms.

With their assignments in hand, further meetings scheduled and their work underway, the meeting adjourned.

# 6

# SUBSEQUENTLY

## THE DEATH COUNT ENDS

Even while the committee went about its work to build a memorial to the dead Arsenal workers, it learned that the death list had expanded. Almost three weeks after the fiery explosion, thirty-one-year-old Pinkey Scott, widowed mother of two, succumbed to the pain of her extensive burns and died on the Fourth of July.

Now familiar with the routine, committee members James King and Joseph Burch arranged for Mrs. Scott's funeral from her Island neighborhood home, near those of Melissa Adams, Sallie McElfresh and Maggie Yonson. With the earth still freshly turned from the June 19 funerals, King and Birch arranged for her to be buried with her "sister sufferers" in the mass grave at Congressional Cemetery. The funeral was held on July 6 in the aftermath of the nation's fireworks-bedecked birthday.

## "RELIEF OF THE SUFFERERS BY A LATE ACCIDENT..."

On the Fourth of July, Congress stepped in to supplement the workers' committee's charitable efforts. Working on the holiday, the House passed a "Joint Resolution for the Relief of the Sufferers by a late Accident at the U.S. Arsenal in Washington, D.C." The resolution, eloquent in its description of the plight of poor workers, is notable for the fact that even though more than two weeks had passed since the explosion, Congress was still unable to correctly state the number of victims. At the time the Congressional

Committee was writing its resolution, the death toll stood at twenty, and Pinkey Scott would die that very evening. The resolution, however, refers to just nineteen deaths. Its introduction reports that

> *nearly thirty persons, mostly females, were terribly injured, nineteen of them fatally, by an explosion in the cartridge factory at the United States arsenal in Washington, D.C., on the seventeenth day of June, eighteen hundred and sixty-four.*

The resolution goes on to describe the economic status of the survivors, saying they are "poor, and dependent upon daily labor for bread, [and] who by this calamity have been deprived of the power to earn their living, and are without the means to procure the care and comfort necessary to their recovery." Against this descriptive background, Congress concluded:

> *Be it resolved by the Senate and House of Representatives of the United States of America in Congress assembled, That the sum of two thousand dollars be, and the same is hereby, appropriated out of any money in the treasury not otherwise appropriated, for the relief of the victims of such explosion—said money to be distributed under the direction of Major Benton, commanding at said arsenal, and in such manner as shall most conduce to the comfort and relief of said sufferers, according to their necessities respectively, and that he report to this house.*

Responding to Congress on December 5, Benton succinctly explained how he distributed the aid. Of the $2,000, $175 went to the guardian of each child orphaned by the disaster. These were George, the son of Emily Collins; Annie and Willie, the two children of Pinkey Scott; and Honorah and Ella, the children of Kate Brosnahan, whom Benton mistakenly refers to as "Breslahan." In total, the seven children received $875.

Catharine Goldsmith, a survivor who was badly burned on the face, hands and arms received $20.00 for medicines; while Anne Cogan, the widowed mother of Catharine, a thirteen-year-old survivor, received $72.44. This award consisted of both a donation and a payment for medicine. The reason why Catharine Cogan deserved a "donation" while Catharine Goldsmith did not is not explained.

Nor is an explanation provided for the $5.81 paid to John R. King for "hack-hire at funeral." No detail is offered as to what distinguished Mr. King's services for payment from this congressional fund. It may be that

Benton's "John R. King" is, in fact, the committeeman "James R. King" who coordinated the funeral of Pinkey Scott. If so, it is not clear why this rather small expense would not have been paid under the separate provisions of Secretary Stanton's directive that the War Department assume all costs related to the Arsenal funeral. Perhaps the reasons were so obvious to an observer of the day that no explanation was deemed necessary. Be that as it may, no explanation was offered, and Congress, satisfied, requested no further detail.

The last major item was $1,026.75 paid to "110 women who lost articles of clothing at the time of the accident." Apparently, the government, quite properly, compensated the women for clothing damaged by the fire. However, the total laboratory workforce was 110 women, suggesting that this clothing allowance included the families of the 21 women who died in the fire and not just the 89 who survived to return to work. Each woman would have gotten about $9.50.

What is perhaps most startling about these allocations is that, with the exception of the contributions to the orphaned children, no money was distributed to the families of the women killed in the explosion. In the absence of specific directions from Congress, Major Benton, as was his prerogative, prioritized the needs as he saw fit. The result was a four-tier priority: 1) children of widowed mothers; 2) women who were seriously burned but did not die from their wounds; 3) replacement of clothing damaged by the fire; and 4) Mr. King's unique hack fare. A justification for not assisting the families of the deceased victims was, apparently, felt unnecessary.

Although harsh by modern standards in which disaster awards of millions of dollars are reported, frugal awards such as these, nonetheless, might have been seen as comforting and appropriate in 1864. It should be noted that it was only a few years earlier, in 1862, that the government started providing pensions to the widows of soldiers killed in battle. In a now seemingly quaint policy, the pension of an unmarried soldier was assigned to his mother and, should she not be alive, to his unmarried sisters. Only in the absence of a wife, mother or sister was the father or brother eligible to receive the pension payment. From Major Benton's perspective, therefore, benefits might have been felt justified only if the deceased was the family's chief breadwinner and her death left no one in the home to take care of the surviving children. Accordingly, since most of the victims were either minor children themselves or wives with surviving spouses—and therefore, not a household's chief wage earner—only widows with minor children would have been seen as the main providers for families that were now incapable of supporting themselves and, therefore, in need of assistance.

Support for this "loss of the breadwinner" theory can be found in Benton's letter to the House of Representatives on June 6, 1866, almost two years after the 1864 disaster. In this letter, Benton reported to Congress on the disbursement of funds to the sufferers of the second Washington Arsenal explosion, this one occurring a year and a half later on December 18, 1865, in which nine were killed and two wounded. None of the victims were women or children.

Providing more detail than his 1864 letter, Benton described the family situation of each victim. The largest award went to Margaret Moran, whose husband had been killed in the explosion. Moran had two children ages two and five. With her husband's death, she was left with no support, no property and, since she was paying rent, no home of her own. She received $400.

Approximately $350.00 was given to Ellen Fealy, the widow of Thomas. In his justification, Benton noted that out of nine children, Mrs. Fealy was still caring for four daughters aged twelve, ten, eight and five. Mitigating her situation, somewhat, was the fact that Mrs. Fealy had two married daughters, as well as two grown sons who made $3.50 per day. In addition, she also owned "two small frame houses and…a small store."

Three other widows each received $300. Two of the women had one young child each, while the third may have been pregnant, a condition inferred from Benton's comment that she had "no family as yet."

The widow of Martin Coyle and the mother of John Meehan both received awards of $250. Mrs. Coyle had an eight-month-old infant and lived with relatives, while Mrs. Meehan, who owned no property and rented her housing, had a working daughter.

The mother of Charles Linn was a widow whose three children were either married or working. Noting that she owned "part of a house in Philadelphia," she was awarded $100. No mention was made of the fact that her dead son had also lost a leg in the war.

The smallest individual awards went to the three sisters of Jeremiah Mahoney. In noting that, although unmarried, each of the sisters was employed as a house servant, or as Benton subtly described them, "living out in serve," each received $33.33.

Although not killed in the blast, John Crane, married and the father of one, was crippled for life. His compensation was $110.

Last on the list was James Lawler. Wounded, "but not so severely as to detain him from work," the property-less Lawler received forty dollars. Although fit to work, Lawler likely was deemed eligible for an award because he had "a father, mother, and sisters principally depending on him for support."

In examining the two awards, the only element of consistency between them seems to be Benton's subjective judgment of the degree to which a household was able to continue as a family in the absence of the dead wage earner's economic contribution. This was no studied policy attempting to compensate a spouse or a parent for the death of a loved one in the cause of public service; rather, it was a subjective attempt by a well-intentioned government functionary to help a distressed family bridge the loss of an element of sustainability. In this context, it was not the loss of life, or the loss of family income per se, that was the key operational factor. Instead, Benton seemed to be asking himself the question, "To what extent is the household able to continue as an economic unit without the victim's wages?" If the family members could not work, were not supported by others and had little or no property, then a "large" award might be justified. Where an ability to provide was present, benefits were deemed neither appropriate nor necessary.

Given the absence of a public response to the government's actions, and the extensive fundraising efforts of the workers' committees, it might safely be inferred that the public expected little of the federal government under such traumatic circumstances. It not being expected, the offer of even minor assistance would have been appreciated and gratefully accepted.

## SAFETY RULES

On July 22, 1864, almost five weeks after the explosion, Major Benton posted a twenty-one-item safety notice in all the laboratory buildings. In light of the events of the past month, the notice is startling in that its first words caution against the use of iron in the construction of laboratory facilities—a wise safety precaution, indeed, but one irrelevant to the events of June 17. It is only at item number eighteen that the declared cause of the explosion is broached and then in a rather circumspect way. Directing that "the preparation of ornamental fireworks is forbidden in or around any buildings where ammunition is prepared," Benton ignored the fact that Superintendent Brown never admitted, nor did either of the inquiries conclude, that the three trays of fireworks were intended for "ornamental" rather than military use. Given the volatile nature of the chemical compound, prudence would demand an absolute ban on the preparation of all such fireworks around any ammunition facility.

Items nineteen ("No other operations than those prescribed by the Commanding Officer of the Arsenal will be allowed in any room or building used for laboratory or magazine purposes.") and twenty-one ("The Officer of the Day and the person in charge of a laboratory will see that these regulations are duly enforced, by promptly reporting any person found violating them."), while certainly germane, nonetheless carry a hint of a self-serving attempt to provide the Arsenal's commandant with a shield of plausible deniability in the event of an accident.

Of the twenty-one items, only five address circumstances that might have prevented, or at least mitigated, the carnage of June 17. In addition to item eighteen, the other four relevant precautions are: item three ("Water and sweep continually during work, particularly in hot dry weather and when loose powder is being handled."), item four ("Put linen blinds to windows exposed to the sun."), item ten ("Never have more powder than necessary in the work shops.") and the first portion of item twenty ("When the operations are considered dangerous, the workmen will be kept separate as far as possible from each other.").

Ironically, while items six, seven and eight require the removal of street footwear and the use of "moccasins" upon entry to the laboratory, the list contains neither a prohibition against the wearing of hoop skirts nor a requirement that clothing be treated with a known flame retardant such as "alum water."

When read against the backdrop of the Arsenal disaster, Benton's efforts to "Prevent Accidents in Laboratories" is a document that easily could have been—and, in fact, may well have been—written prior to the June 17 explosion. If any lessons were learned from this disaster, evidence is absent from this notice.

## "A HANDSOME AND SUBSTANTIAL MONUMENT…"

Within a month of starting its work, the monument committee had subscriptions totaling over $2,000. Committee representatives made it known, however, that as appreciative as they were of the donations to date, another thousand dollars were still needed. In a July 22 news item, King and Burch expressed their hope that "the citizens generally (as opposed to just Arsenal and government workers) will subscribe, and enable them to raise a handsome and substantial monument to mark the spot where eighteen [*sic*] of the twenty-one unfortunate victims rest."

As admirable as were their sentiments, this article was the first in what would be a long train of confusion about how many victims were buried in the Congressional Cemetery mass grave. Fifteen remains lay at the site where the memorial was to be constructed: the eight unidentified and six known victims buried in the two graves on Sunday, June 19, plus Pinkey Scott, who was buried on July 5. Sallie McElfresh and Annie Bache were also buried at Congressional, but each in separate family plots. Four of the victims had chosen to be buried in the Catholic cemetery of Mount Olivet. Fortunately, media misstatements posed no stumbling block to the committee's fundraising efforts. On July 27, committeeman George Collison reported that he had collected over $600.00 from various associations, including Lodge #10 of the International Order of Odd Fellows ($25.00); the Tenth Precinct of the Metropolitan Police, the unit that had provided so much help in maintaining order on the day of the funeral ($22.20); the carpenters working on the treasury extension near the White House ($26.25); and the Navy Yard ship carpenters ($75.00). Mr. Collison was confident that other groups with which he had contact were keen to do their part.

By the end of October, the $3,000 goal had been reached, and Dudley immediately posted advertisements soliciting design proposals in the papers of Washington, Baltimore and Philadelphia.

Setting a seemingly impossibly tight deadline of November 19, the ad solicited design proposals for a monument and a fence to enclose it. The workers were very specific about what they wanted. The monument was to be made of American white marble, list the names of the twenty-one victims and include the date of the accident. Perhaps reflecting the fact that the proposal was developed by craftsmen who understood both materials and the building process, the advertisement specified that the successful design was to be built on a granite slab, six feet square and two and a half feet deep, laid in cement. Leaving little to chance, the committee also specified that the design include a fence to be made of cast iron, rest on "suitable blocks of granite" and enclose a space eighteen feet by fifteen feet. The bidders also were to state how long it would take to complete the project. Costs were limited to $3,000, and the work was "to be executed to the satisfaction of the committee." Bidders could submit their proposals to any one of four committee members—Joseph Burch, John Dudley, James R. King or James Johnson—care of the Washington Arsenal.

## LOT FLANNERY'S WORK

By the deadline, nineteen designs had been received from Hartford, New York, Baltimore and Washington. The award was given not to an established sculptor but rather to the Washington stonecutting firm of Flannery &

Flannery & Brothers' Washington City Directory advertisement. *Courtesy of the Washington, D.C. Public Library, Washingtoniana Division.*

Brothers. The design, described as "a very handsome one," varied slightly from the published specifications. Rather than using American white marble, the Flannerys substituted Italian marble. It would be twenty-five feet high, include the names of the victims and capped with a "statue of Grief." The brothers promised to have the work done by May 15.

The Flannerys were brothers, Lot (b. 1836) and Martin (b. 1844), both of whom had immigrated to Washington from Limerick, Ireland, as young men. They operated a successful stonecutting business on Massachusetts Avenue that specialized in funeral monuments. Lot, however, had ambitions to a status of something more than just a stonecutter. He saw himself as an artist and, as such, would gain notoriety as a sculptor in postwar Washington. The Arsenal Monument would be the cornerstone on which he would build a reputation and a successful career.

Visually elegant and simple, the Flannery creation is in fact a complex and detailed creation. There is a six-foot square foundation of blue rock edged

The Arsenal Monument.
*Photo by Brian Bergin.*

with a course of finished granite. Resting on this is a base of Baltimore County marble, five and a half feet square and two feet high. On this stands an Italian marble pediment, holding four die blocks at each compass point: on the east and west panels are the names of all the victims, and not just those who rest under the monument; to the south, or the front side, is a bas-relief representation of the laboratory engulfed in smoke and flames and the inscription:

> *Killed*
> *By An Explosion*
> *At The U.S. Arsenal*
> *Washington, D.C.*
> *June 17ᵗʰ 1864*

The Arsenal Monument front inscription. *Photo by Brian Bergin.*

On the north-facing panel is another inscription:

*Erected*
*By Public Contributions*
*By the Citizens Of*
*Washington, D.C.*
*June 17ᵗʰ 1865*

The pediment head mourns the fleetness of time with carved acanthus leaves and winged hourglasses, common nineteenth-century symbols of death that most mourners would have recognized as representations of an untimely death. From this base rises a ten-foot paneled shaft with ornate edges carved to mimic the fold of crape. A stylized ivy vine entwines the sides of the summit stone upon which stands the poignant figure of Flannery's *Grief*.

Life-sized, the statue of a young woman stands with a slight rightward tilt to her head. With tear-drained eyes downcast, she forlornly gazes through

*Grief*, by Lot Flannery. *Photo by Brian Bergin.*

the sod, seeking the spirits of the spent young lives lying burned and buried beneath her towering roost. Fashionably curled hair, hanging freely, curtains the back of a full-length, waist-cinched smock. She has paused mid-stride, her leading right leg accented by the backwashed folds of swaying fabric. And it is here, in the subtle detail of the leg, that Lot Flannery's intent becomes clear. She is, after all, not one of the victims but one of the survivors. Her dress, loose and long, is not hooped and massive like theirs. Once, perhaps, she glided unhindered around the flames and burning obstacles that touched and torched the aisle-wide skirts of her dead sisters. Now, she gently strolls on sacred soil. And standing on that same ground, too far away in both time and distance to hear, all visitors with grieving hearts know…she sings:

> *Sisters, thou wast mild and lovely*
> *Gentle as the summer breeze…*
> *Farewell sisters, farewell…*

# 7

# AFTERWARD AND OVER TIME

The Flannerys had done their job well, and for years the monument helped. It soothed the wounded hearts of parents and siblings, connected the disrupted lives of husbands and lovers and touched the void of motherless children. But as the winged sands of time claimed family members, childhood friends and all those with a direct memory, purposeful visits to the monument were increasingly replaced with brief encounters by strangers happening by. In the recollections of old-timers and near-decade anniversaries, newspapers would recapitulate the events of June 17, 1864. A published picture of the elegant monument would temporarily astonish a growing population increasingly unconnected to, and unfamiliar with, any descendants of the distraught families or survivors of the disastrous explosion. No truth-seeking investigation ever brought light to the source of the combustion that sparked the wrath of the fiery serpent. Nor did any bestselling author or blockbuster movie ever hold the nation's interest transfixed on the pathos surrounding the twenty-one tragic deaths. A centennial came and went unnoticed, even while the aging, monument-bedecked lawns of Congressional Cemetery increasingly suffered the vandalism and neglect of an indifferent community.

Fortunately, the indifference came to an end in 1976, when District citizens, concerned with the plight of Congressional Cemetery and its thousands of funerary treasures, formed the Association for the Preservation of Historic Congressional Cemetery (APHCC), a nonprofit organization to protect and maintain the remarkable site. Through memberships, donations, fees and

One panel of names of the victims of the Arsenal explosion. *Photo by Brian Bergin.*

grants, the APHCC's board stopped the degradation of the cemetery and has made significant restorative efforts.

A cadre of informed docents is now available to guide visitors through the burial grounds to its many historic plots. Tours regularly include a respectful stop at the Arsenal Monument for a sensitive retelling of the long-ago tragedy. Furthermore, in a unique cooperative effort with the National Parks Service, the APHCC has arranged for the Park Service's preservation crews to refurbish its most prized monuments. In the fall of 2008, some 140 years after the tragedy of that long-ago hot June day, restoration was begun on Lot Flannery's testament to *Grief*. Thanks to the dedication of the APHCC, its storytelling docents and the skills of the National Park Service restorative staff, the restless spirits of long-dead family and friends of the Arsenal women can now rest assured knowing that the names and stories of their daughters are not to be forgotten.

## CONCLUSION

In this narrative of tragedy, we see the efforts of survivors to ensure that a story dear to them would not be forgotten. The victims of the explosion could have been buried in separate funerals and in individual graves. But the families and friends of these dead women clearly wanted something more. They worked hard and sacrificed dearly to ensure that this tragedy and these women would not be forgotten.

# Civil War Disaster in the Capital

In 1864, the Arsenal workers and the residents of the Island were shocked and saddened by the explosion that suddenly and unexpectedly took the lives of twenty-one of their daughters. Keeping with the customs of the day, they expressed their sorrow and grief to the families of the victims individually and collectively as best their meager resources and war-torn emotions allowed.

Gestures of emotional support and financial assistance to each of the victims' families were all the love and custom expected from friends and neighbors. It would have been acceptable for the concerned community to simply help bury the dead and comfort the living. And indeed, we know this was done with tact and efficiency. But notably, it was not all that was done. Clearly, those affected and interested felt that the significance of this incident was such that it should never be forgotten. They were not content to just sympathize; they also felt, very strongly, the need to memorialize. But where lay the significance? What was it that the grieved and grieving saw as uniquely important for all time in this tragedy?

Likely, it was not in the persona of the women individually or their social contribution as a group. Like their families, friends and Island neighbors, the women were common and, in all aspects, considered noteworthy at the time, unremarkable. Whether due to age or circumstance, none had done deeds, either ill natured or good willed, on which the community felt compelled to remark. Most were so ordinary that acquaintances could not accurately brief reporters on their first names, where they lived or how to spell their surnames.

Nor was it just the numbers involved, since they were insignificant when compared to the battlefield death tolls enumerated regularly in the papers.

By themselves, it was not the ages of the victims, since, other than occasional uses of the word "girls" in newspaper accounts, their ages were never mentioned. No, rather than any one element, these deaths were deemed extraordinary for a novel combination of reasons.

First, all the victims were female, and this stood in marked contrast to the daily rolls of young men maimed and murdered in the fury of war. In addition, this was a very different circumstance than the more familiar deaths experienced by women in childbirth, from accidents on the public byways, raging epidemics or domestic abuse.

Second, they were mostly young—many younger even than the soldiers regularly cut down on those many Southern battlefields. Even without the ages of the victims published in the papers, most people of the time would have known that cartridge production was the type of work generally done by children. Although seldom mentioned, "young" would likely have had the concomitant term "innocent" subconsciously appended to it, suggesting that all right-thinking persons would surely see these deaths as both cruel and unjust.

Third, the victims died working to help their distressed families. Work was the common element that brought, and held, the women in that wrong place at that wrong time. All died doing their part to help hold together struggling families. These women were not working outside the home by choice. They were not huddled at the Arsenal for twelve hours a day just so the family could afford an extended vacation, cover tuition at a local private school or purchase a larger home. Instead, it would have been widely appreciated that they were working to provide desperately needy families with a marginal amount of money that would help a widowed mother or their fatherless children survive another day at the economic margin.

Fourth, there were a large number of victims killed in one place, at one time. Scale, as with historic battles, marked this as a memorable event.

Lastly, there was the inherent horror of death by fire. Our primeval revulsion to conflagration, with its religious allusion to damnation, would have earned this accident a high ranking in the annals of nineteenth-century horror. Regardless of superstition or instinct, however, the frequency of accidental burnings in a community housed in wooden shanties and dangerously dependent on coal stoves and kerosene lanterns would have made the agony of the burn victims a firsthand reality known to many through observance, care giving or painful experience.

But even if this tragic story was important to the Island residents and D.C. citizens in 1864 for these reasons or others, the question remains: why should anyone today care about an event some 140 years in the past?

In Stanley Krubric's classic film *2001: A Space Odyssey*, astronauts find a sleek, black obelisk on the moon's surface that, when touched, sends a signal to an unknown, and assumedly distant, civilization. The obelisk had been purposefully planted so that one civilization could communicate with another that it had never met. Some similar act of blind communication can be appreciated at the Washington Arsenal memorial. There, in Congressional Cemetery, visitors—be they astronauts, explorers or tourists—will discover Flannery's obelisk-like creation, positioned as if purposefully left behind by a now-departed civilization in an attempt to deliver a message to peoples it would never meet.

A respectful visit to the monument, involving a silent reading of the front and back etched plaques and the flanking tablets listing the twenty-one names, might reasonably conclude with a thoughtful contemplation of the significance of the sculpted survivor atop the monument, perpetually grieving for friends denied the joys of a fully lived life. Stepping forward slightly and reaching out gently, a visitor's delicate touch against the monument's roughhewn surface might seem to generate an emotional spark that telegraphs a silent message

Female Arsenal workers. *The Washington Arsenal Manufactory Women Killed in the Explosion, (circa 1864). Courtesy of the National Archives and Records Administration, College Park, Maryland, Still Photo Division.*

of empathy with the mourners of those long-ago lost souls. For it is only in the contemplation of the monument that the modern observer begins to understand the subliminal message sent to us by those whose tears and penny-ante contributions generated it. With an appreciation for the narrative, and in emotional proximity to the monument, we today are prepared to understand that in 1864, their grief was too much to be borne by one generation, and through cut and drafted stone, they hoped to dilute their anguish by spreading their sorrow across time. When remembering their tragedy and visiting their monument, we of other generations send a message that we are neither too remote nor too preoccupied in our own time to understand why, in a now distant day, a burden-laden president and a broken-hearted people saw their heavens hung in black.

*Farewell Sisters, Farewell*

# EPILOGUE

*The following epilogue was written by Michael Fritsch, whose ancestors adopted Kate Brosnahan's two orphans from the Arsenal explosion.*

Like many people, I have long had an interest in genealogy and history. Years ago, when my uncle told me my grandparents were second cousins, I was more than a little curious. He told me they weren't related by blood but through adoption. My great-great-grandmother, Honorah Brosnahan, was adopted after her parents died in the Civil War. My uncle mentioned it had something to do with an arsenal explosion in South Washington. These dramatic revelations stirred me to learn more about my ancestors and what influences this catastrophe had on my family.

Honorah and her sister, Ella, were the daughters of Thomas Brosnahan. Thomas lived with his wife, Kate, and their young ones on C Street Southwest, just a few blocks from the fetid stench of the Washington City Canal. A poor shoemaker, Thomas struggled to provide for his family.

Thomas was aware there were limited opportunities for him, the war being one of them. By 1863, enthusiasm among the volunteers to fight had worn thin, and the Union draft was put in place that summer. To avoid the brutality of war, drafted wealthy men paid others more than three hundred dollars to take their place. This amount was equivalent to how much a man like Thomas could earn in a year. Thomas was desperate and determined, and he joined the battles as a substitute soldier. Precious in his eyes, Kate and their girls were worth his peril. The money would make life more comfortable for them, but sadly not so much so that Kate could stay home with their children.

After Thomas left, Kate's life as a single mother was not easy. Kate found employment at the Arsenal, which was within walking distance of their home. There she worked at a monotonous job in stifling heat. Joking and small talk to ease the oppressiveness were not allowed. While she labored, Kate undoubtedly contemplated the infrequent letters received from Thomas and wondered if she would ever hear from him again. She did have relatives living nearby to whom she could turn but found them unreliable. She didn't even have them watch her girls during the day and instead entrusted them to a domestic.

Surely, Kate knew how dangerous her task at the Arsenal was. It is likely she was attracted to the above-average wages, justifiable because of the risks. Dozens of workers had already died or were maimed in Civil War ordnance work, but most of the hundreds who assembled explosives were fine. Perhaps it was a little easier taking those risks knowing the cartridges she assembled may have been on their way to her husband.

On the morning of the explosion, as she walked down 4½ Street to work, Kate probably thought about her children and felt anguished to hear little Ella cry as she left. Or perhaps she held out hope that everyone was wrong about Thomas's demise, that he would soon be home and they would be a family again. Dark thoughts were pushed away once more, knowing that working to stave off poverty for her children was what she needed to focus on.

The Arsenal explosion shook the ground of Washington and reverberated throughout the entire district. These deaths were not those of prepared soldiers in some far-off battlefield but mothers, wives and sisters just working for the day. These unexpected deaths were most devastating and demanded an outpouring of sympathy in reply. The citizens of Washington extended their response beyond the days of the funeral; there were orphans in need of support.

Sometime after the explosion, and with Thomas assumed dead, William and Mary Schwing adopted Kate's daughters. The Schwings were a young couple who were just starting out. They had faith that a new restaurant William had recently opened would eventually secure their future. Even though William was putting in long hours, he and Mary felt they were able to devote loving attention to the foundlings. The Schwings' benevolence changed the girls' lives. Because of the Schwings, Honorah and Ella had a stable and nurturing home and a place to heal. The girls would grow to understand how to care for families of their own.

The sisters also learned through example that caring for others was what was expected. Having other responsibilities was no excuse to avoid involvement with their neighbors. As their fortunes grew, the entire family was often mentioned in the Washington papers, frequently referencing their philanthropic activities. William even testified on behalf of the Washington Humane Society, as a witness in an animal cruelty case involving a horse. The family was always sharing what they had with those who had little, joining others to right social ills and fighting for the defenseless.

Stories about those involved in the Arsenal disaster offer an account of our ancestors and the influence of a misfortune on an entire community. Because of the magnitude of the event, it is easy to see the values expressed by those involved. These people made sacrifices for their spouses and children, suffering for the greater good. They worked hard at dangerous jobs. It is heartening to be reminded of those who risked their lives to make things better for their families and even more inspiring to learn about the resilient ones who were willing to love the strangers left behind, share their sorrow and bring them into their families. Each generation has its hurdles and challenges that must be overcome. These stories show where we come from and our inheritance as a people. These are the values passed down to our generation: sacrifice, hard work and generosity. Our ancestors didn't have to go to war, bear dangerous jobs or open their homes to outsiders. They chose those things because they were the right things to do and the fullest expressions of their humanity.

Michael R. Fritsch, PhD
Detroit, July 18, 2012

# Notes

1. The National Unity Party was an expedient coalition of Republicans and those Democrats who supported the war.
2. See John L. Carnprobst, "Tragedy at the U.S. Allegheny Arsenal," 42–43, for a description of an alternative packing arrangement.
3. Author's calculation based on Thomas's report of 1,420,000 cartridges produced for the quarter ending June 30, 1864, and an assumption of sixty-six workdays in that quarter.
4. The C.W. Evans article provides an informative and more complimentary profile of Mr. Baker.
5. Also known as Howard M. per the *Evening Star*, June 18, 1864.
6. A review of the 1860 federal census confirms that at least five of the twelve jury members were employed in these occupations.
7. It is assumed that the blast blew the doors closed. Previous testimony mentioned that all the doors were open. Also, given the summer heat, it would not be unreasonable to conclude that the doors, like the windows, were open.

# BIBLIOGRAPHY

Adams, George Worthington. *Doctors in Blue: The Medical History of the Union Army in the Civil War*. Baton Rouge: Louisiana State University Press, 1952.

Adjutant General's Office. *Special Orders No. 210*. Washington, D.C.: War Department, 1864.

Aldrich, R.D., and C.J. McKusick. "Ammunition Fires—Shooting Away Misconceptions." *Fire Engineering* (1984): 14–16.

Anderson, Joseph, DD, and Anna L. Ward, eds. *The Town and City of Waterbury, Connecticut from the Aboriginal Period to the Year Eighteen Hundred and Ninety-five*. Vol. II. New Haven, CT: The Price & Lee Company, 1869.

Association for the Preservation of Historic Congressional Cemetery. "E" Street SE. Washington, D.C., 1801. www.congressionalcemetery.org.

———. McElfresh interment information, n.d.

Basler, R.P., ed. *The Collected Works of Abraham Lincoln*. Vol. 7. Springfield, IL: The Abraham Lincoln Association, 1953.

Becer, Allan. The Allegheny Arsenal. 1998. Originally available at http://www.contrib.andrew.cmu.edu/~jw3u/round/arsenal.htm.

Benton, J.G. *Letter from Major Benton, Commandant of the Washington Arsenal, Transmitting a Statement of the Distribution of Money to the Sufferers by the Late Explosion in Said Arsenal, Ordnance Bureau*. Washington, D.C., 1866.

———. *Letter from Major J.G. Benton Reporting the Disbursements of Funds Appropriated for the Relief of Sufferers by Accident at the Arsenal at Washington City, Ordnance Bureau*. Washington, D.C., 1864.

———. *Maj. Benton Gives an Official Report, in Detail, of the Accident which Occurred at this Post on the 17th Inst. (June 18, 1864)*. Washington, D.C., 1864.

Bergin, Brian. "Tragedy at City's Arsenal: Explosion Kills 21 Women." *Washington Times*, May 17, 2008.

Boatner, Mark Mayo, III. *The Civil War Dictionary*. New York: Vintage Books, 1991.

Boyd, Andrew. *Boyd's Washington and Georgetown Directory Containing also a Business Directory of Washington, Georgetown and Alexandria*. Washington, D.C.: Hudson Taylor, 1864.

Boyd, Wm. H. *Boyd's Directory of Washington & Georgetown Together with a Business Directory of Alexandria, VA and a Compendium of their Government, Institutions, and Trades*. Washington, D.C.: Boyd's Directory Co., 1867.

Burton, D.L. "Friday the 13th: Richmond's Great Home Front Disaster." *Civil War Times Illustrated* (1982): 36–41.

Carnprobst, J.L. "Tragedy at the U.S. Allegheny Arsenal." *Blue & Gray* (1985): 28–43.

Casey, S. *Report in Compliance with S.O. 210 Conc'g the Explosion which Occurred Today at the Washington Arsenal*. Washington, D.C., 1864.

Congressional Cemetery Burial Log. Jenks log entry. Washington, D.C., 1864.

*Daily Dispatch*. "Gunpowder Explosion and Loss of Life." March 14, 1863.

———. "The Late Dreadful Explosion on Brown's Island." March 16, 1863.

*Daily Morning Chronicle*. "The Arsenal Calamity (Church Sevices)." June 23, 1864.

———. "The Arsenal (Clean-up)." June 25, 1864.

———. "Cleanliness—Bathing." June 27, 1864.

———. "Friday's Tragedy." June 20, 1864.

———. "Madame Kretschmar Sacred Concert." June 20, 1864.

———. "President Leaves Philadelphia." June 18, 1864.

———. "Sad Result." June 21, 1864.

———. "State of the Thermometer." June 18, 1864.

*Daily National Intelligencer*. "The Calamity at the Arsenal." June 20, 1864.

———. "Fire at the Watervleit Arsenal (NY)." June 21, 1864.

———. "The President's Visit to Philadelphia." June 18, 1864.

———. "The Sacred Concert." June 20, 1864.

———. "A Sad Affair." June 20, 1864.

———. "A Sad Result." June 21, 1864.

———. "Terrible Calamity." June 18, 1864.

*Daily National Republican*. "Saved by Her Tongue." June 20, 1864.

Evans, C.W. "Lafayette Baker and Security in the Civil War North." *North & South* (September 2008): 44–51.

*Evening Star.* "An Afflicted Family." June 20, 1864.

―――. "Another." June 21, 1864.

―――. "Another Victim." July 5, 1864.

―――. "The Arsenal Accident—Funeral Obsequies." June 24, 1864.

―――. "The Arsenal Disaster." June 20, 1864.

―――. "The Arsenal Grounds, Some More Reminiscences by an Old Resident; The Great Explosion and Fire Recalled— Mr. Shackleford's Heroism." December 27, 1902.

―――. "Arsenal Explosion—Disaster of Nearly Forty Years Ago—A Monument Erected—Twenty-one Girls in Laboratory Burned to Death—President Lincoln and Secretary Stanton Attend Funeral—Greatest Fatality in City." February 20, 1904.

―――. "Arsenal Improvements." November 4, 1864.

―――. "Compensation of Clerks." January 4, 1865.

―――. "Dead Horses." March 22, 1865.

―――. "Died: John Carter Brown Jenckes." June 18, 1864.

―――. "Died: Rebecca Hull." June 18, 1864.

―――. "A Difficulty at the Funeral." June 20, 1864.

―――. "The Explosion Yesterday at the Arsenal; Further Details and Particulars—The Coroner's Inquest." June 18, 1864.

―――. "Fire in the Watervleit Arsenal." June 18, 1864.

―――. "Found in the Canal." May 25, 1865.

―――. "Frightful Explosion at the Arsenal." June 17, 1864.

―――. "Funeral Expenses." June 21, 1864.

―――. "The Funeral of the Victims of the Arsenal Explosion; Affecting Scenes; Interesting Obsequies &c." June 20, 1864.

―――. "Further Particulars of the Explosion; More of the Bodies Recognized; Preparation for Interment." June 18, 1864.

―――. "Further Particulars of the Terrible Explosion at the Arsenal." June 17, 1864.

―――. "A Good Move." June 21, 1864.

―――. "Hot." June 25, 1864.

―――. "Letter re: Wages of Government Clerks." January 2, 1865.

―――. "Mad Dogs." May 1, 1865.

―――. "Meeting of the Employees of the Arsenal." June 20, 1864.

―――. "The Monument to the Arsenal Victims." March 23, 1865.

―――. "Monument to the Arsenal Victims." July 19, 1914.

―――. "The Monument to the Victims of the Explosion at the Arsenal." July 22, 1864.

———. "Monument to the Victims of June 17ᵗʰ." November 26, 1864.

———. "Noted Sculptor Claimed by Death." December 19, 1922.

———. "President Lincoln and the Philadelphia Fair." June 16, 1864.

———. "The President's Visit to Philadelphia." June 17, 1864.

———. "Proposals Will Be Received Until Saturday." November 3, 1864.

———. "The Relief and Monument Fund for the Sufferers by the Arsenal Accident." July 27, 1864.

———. "Salaries of Government Clerks." January 10, 1865.

———. "Scalds and Burns." October 12, 1864.

———. "State of the Thermometer." June 20, 1864.

———. "Stealing the Side Walks." February 23, 1865.

———. "The Victims of the Arsenal Disaster." October 29, 1864.

———. "The Wages at the Navy Yard." February 24, 1865.

———. "Wages Raised." September 17, 1864.

———. "Washington's Most Fearful Accident." December 25, 1902.

Faust, Drew Gilpin. *This Republic of Suffering: Death and the American Civil War.* New York: Alfred A. Knopf, 2008.

Foote, Shelby. *The Civil War: A Narrative—Fredericksburg to Meridian.* New York: Random House, 1963.

———. *The Civil War: A Narrative—Red River to Appomattox.* New York: Random House, 1974.

Furgurson, Ernest B. *Freedom Rising: Washington in the Civil War.* New York: Alfred A. Knopf, 2004.

Goodwin, Doris Kearns. *Team of Rivals: The Political Genius of Abraham Lincoln.* New York: Simon & Schuster, 2005.

Heidler, D.S., and J.T. Heidler, eds. *Encyclopedia of the American Civil War: A Political, Social, and Military History.* New York: W.W. Norton & Company, 2000.

Howell, H. Grady, Jr. *The Most Appalling Disaster: Jackson, Mississippi Arsenal Explosion, November 5, 1862.* 2008. Originally available at http://battleofraymond.org/howell.htm.

Johns, Cliff. "Memorial to Tragedy of June 17, 1864." *Washington Times,* February 23, 2002.

*Joint Resolution for the Relief of the Suffers by a Late Accident at the U.S. Arsenal in Washington, D.C.* Washington, D.C., 1864.

Kansier, Jim, fire marshall (ret.). Interview, Monroe, MI, 2008.

Kosanke, Ken. Interview. "Red and White Star Fireworks." Whitewater, CO, 2008.

Kubric, Stanley, and Arthur C. Clark. *2001: A Space Odyssey.* Metro-Goldwyn-Mayer, Turner Entertainment, Warner Bros., 1968.

Leech, Margaret. *Reveille in Washington, 1860–1865*. New York: Harper & Brothers, 1941.

Massey, Mary Elizabeth. *Women in the Civil War*. Lincoln: University of Nebraska Press, 1996.

McClellan, P.I. *Silent Sentinel on the Potomac*. New York: Heritage Books, Inc., 1993.

McFeely, Mary Drake, and William S. McFeely, eds. *Grant: Memoirs and Selected Letters*. Literary Classics of the United States. New York: Southern Illinois University Press, 1990.

McPherson, James M. *Battle Cry of Freedom: The Civil War Era*. New York: Oxford University Press, 1988.

Mt. Olivet Cemetery. 1300 Bladensberg Road NE. Washington, D.C.

Nazarov, Amy Rogers. "Arsenal Monument Marks a Sad Tale—Lives of Women Forever Memorialized." *Hill Rag* (June 2006).

*The Papers of Abraham Lincoln, 1861–1864*. "Funerals." Originally available at http://www.stg.brown.edu/projects/lincoln/search.php.

Proctor, John Clagett. "Grief Written by Tragedies." *Sunday Star*, April 28, 1935.

Ramsay, G.D. *Letter to Secretary of War re: The Hours of Labor at Arsenals, etc. (May 8, 1864)*. Washington, D.C., 1864.

Schneider, A. Gregory. "Methodism." In *The Oxford Companion to United States History*, edited by P.S. Boyer. New York: Oxford University Press, Inc., 2001.

Simpson, Brooks D. *Ulysses S. Grant: Triumph Over Adversity, 1822–1865*. New York: Houghton Mifflin Company, 2000.

Smith, S.F., and L. Mason. "Sister, Thou Wast Mild and Lovely." In *Hymns and Tune Book for the Church and the Home*. N.p.: American Unitarian Association, 1831.

Spinnenweber, Lawrence J., Jr. "Pittsburgh's Bloodiest Day." Civil War Interactive Blue and Gray Daily. http://www.civilwarinteractive.com.

Stanton, E.M. *Letter to H.W. Halleck, Chief of Staff of the Army re: Inquiry into Washington Arsenal Explosion*. Washington, D.C., 1864.

———. *Telegram to Major Benton re: Funeral Expenses (June 19, 1864)*. Washington, D.C., 1864.

Staudenraus, P.J., ed. *Mr. Lincoln's Washington: Selections from the Writing of Noah Brooks Civil War Correspondent*. New York: Thomas Yoseloff, 1967.

Thomas, Dean S. *Round Ball to Rimfire: A History of Civil War Small Arms Ammunition*. Part I. Gettysburg, PA: Thomas Publication, 1997.

United States Federal Census. Adams, Melissa. Ward #6, District of Columbia. 1860.

———. Arnold, Ann. Ward #7, District of Columbia. 1860.

———. Arnold (Tippett), Emma. Ward #7, District of Columbia. 1860.

———. Bache, Annie. District of Columbia. 1860.

———. Baird, Emily. Ward #6, District of Columbia. 1860.

———. Brahler, Elizabeth. Ward #6, District of Columbia. 1860.

———. Brown, Thomas B. Ward #6, District of Columbia. 1860.

———. Brown, Thomas B. Ward #7, District of Columbia. 1870.

———. Burch, Joseph A. Ward #6, District of Columbia. 1860.

———. Cogan, Catharine. Ward #4, District of Columbia. 1870.

———. Collins, Emily (Martha E.). District of Columbia. 1860.

———. Connor, Johanna. Ward #4, District of Columbia. 1860.

———. Dudley, Henry. Ward #6, District of Columbia. 1860.

———. Greenfield, Henry. Ward #6, District of Columbia. 1870.

———. Greenfield, James H. Ward #6, District of Columbia. 1860.

———. Greenwell, William H. Ward #6, District of Columbia. 1860.

———. Gunnell, Sarah. Ward #6, District of Columbia. 1860

———. Harris, Susan. Ward #4, District of Columbia. 1860.

———. Horan, Catherine. 1860, Ward: 6: District of Columbia.

———. Kidwell, Sarah E. Ward #7, District of Columbia. 1860.

———. Leach, Samuel V. Washington, D.C. 1910.

———. McElfresh, John. Ward #7, District of Columbia. 1850.

———. McElfresh, Sallie. Ward #6, District of Columbia. 1860.

———. Mitchell, Wilhimina. Ward #6, District of Columbia. 1860.

———. Roach, Ellen (aka Roche). Ward #4, District of Columbia. 1860.

———. Seufferle, Henry W. Ward #6, District of Columbia. 1860.

———. Thomas, G. Clinton. Ward #7, District of Columbia. 1850.

———. Webster, Willie A. Ward #7, District of Columbia, 1850.

———. Wise, William D. Ward #7, Washington, D.C. 1850.

———. Woodward, Thomas. Ward #2, District of Columbia. 1860.

*Washington Herald.* "Requiem Mass Tomorrow for Lot Flannery, 86." December 20, 1922.

*Washington Post.* "Lott Flannery, Noted Sculptor, Dies at 86." December 20, 1922.

Williams, David. *A People's History of the Civil War: Struggles for the Meaning of Freedom.* New York: The New Press, 2005.

Worley, W.R. "Guns and Bullets in Fires." *Fire Engineering* (1988): 12–13.

Wunderlich, George C. Executive Director, National Museum of Civil War Medicine. Interview. Frederick, MD, 2007.

# Index

# ABOUT THE AUTHOR

A Peace Corps volunteer, a Vietnam veteran, a teacher and employee of the AFL-CIO, Brian Bergin's life was a multitude of experiences. A constant in his life was a love of learning and a deep affection for history. Over the course of several years, he re-created Lewis and Clark's journey from Missouri to Oregon, keeping a diary of conditions along his route. He biked the C&O Canal from Cumberland, Maryland, back to his home in Arlington, Virginia, because he was fascinated with the history of the canal and how it was constructed. He often hiked in Shenandoah National Park, going there almost every weekend when he was learning about the Civilian Conservation Corps. But the Civil War was his favorite era. Taking him to any battlefield was always a special experience because he could make you see the battle unfold before your eyes. He loved to tell a good story.

*Photo by Brian Bergin.*

Originally from Grand Rapids, Michigan, he lived in Harrisonburg, Virginia, at the time of his death in 2009.

# ABOUT THE EDITOR

Erin Bergin Voorheis is a wife and mother of four. She has a degree in English from Washington State University and, in addition to owning her own home-based business, she is a freelance technical writer and editor. She is currently reading her way through the *New York Times* Best 100 Novels. She lives in Leesburg, Virginia.